Cut & Paste Mini-Books

MATH

NANCY I. SANDERS

New York • Toronto • London • Auckland • Sydney
Mexico City • New Delhi • Hong Kong • Buenos Aires

Teaching
Resources

To Mr. Darl Sams, from Everett Area High School, who taught me to enjoy the exciting challenge of math. Thanks for your commitment to teaching and shaping growing minds!

To Mrs. Elizabeth England, from Everett Area High School, who encouraged me to sew my brother a three-piece suit and, in doing so, taught me to dream big dreams and accomplish more than anyone thought possible! Thank you for your inspiration and dedication as a Home Economics teacher.

Edited by Immacula A. Rhodes
Cover design by Jason Robinson
Interior illustrations by Lucia Kemp Henry
Interior design by Holly Grundon

ISBN-13: 978-0-439-60630-1
ISBN-10: 0-439-60630-6

Contents

Introduction

Welcome *to Cut & Paste Mini-Books: Math!* These 15 mini-books raise the use of manipulatives to a fun and educational level. Designed to enhance your curriculum, the stories reinforce important standards-based math and literacy skills as children read the text and glue patterns onto the corresponding pages to demonstrate comprehension.

In the mini-books, you'll find a collection of math-driven stories that include high-frequency words and controlled vocabulary. The text is just right for helping beginning readers build word recognition, fluency, and other literacy skills. Built-in math concepts align with the National Council of Teachers of Mathematics (NCTM) standards and curriculum focal points for Kindergarten and first grade, giving children practice in essential math skills such as counting, patterning, adding, subtracting, telling time, and problem solving. Each story prompts children to think about a specific math concept and then respond by gluing patterns onto the pages to complete the book.

Everything you need to make the mini-books is here. As children follow the directions to assemble the books, they'll also get practice in sequencing and building fine motor skills. Each reproducible mini-book includes patterns that children cut out and paste onto the pages. Suggestions for introducing the featured math concepts are provided to help you prepare children to complete the mini-book successfully. The extension activities let you take the skill a step further to help reinforce it.

Children will love revisiting these stories again and again. As they read, they'll enjoy practicing key math skills in a fun, unique way. In addition, children will gain confidence in word recognition and reading fluency with repeated readings. But don't keep all the fun at school—encourage children to take the mini-books home, where they can continue and share the learning excitement with their families!

Using the Mini-Books

Once children have assembled their mini-books, you might walk them through the pages as a preview before they glue the pieces in place. Here are some suggestions for doing this:

❋ Ask children to cut out and place all of the patterns face-up near their mini-book.

❋ Beginning with the cover, read aloud the text on each page.

❋ If a page has a blank for children to fill in, talk about what they need to do to find the number that goes in the blank. At this time, you might talk them through the problem solving and help them arrive at the answer, but tell them not to fill in the blank yet.

❋ As you preview each right-hand page, encourage children to use clues from the text on the spread to decide which pattern belongs on the page. Invite them to place the pattern on the page (but not glue it down yet), and then read the text again. Does the pattern make sense with the text? When finished, ask them to put the pattern back with the others.

❋ When you preview page 11 of the mini-book (the last page), talk about what children need to do to complete the activity. If desired, work together to find the answers, but tell children to wait until later to fill in the answers.

❋ After previewing the min-book together, have children read it by themselves. This time, ask them to fill in the blanks, glue each pattern to its corresponding page, and complete the activity on page 11.

Assembling the Mini-Books

The cut-and-paste mini-books require very few materials, and children can complete them at their desk or at a learning center. To get started, provide children with copies of the reproducible pages for the selected mini-book, then demonstrate the steps below. (Or you might assemble the books in advance.)

Materials

❋ scissors

❋ crayons or markers

❋ glue stick or paste

❋ stapler

1. Fold the front cover/page 1 in half along the solid center line. Keep the fold to the right side.

2. Repeat step 1 for each of the remaining page pairs: pages 2/3, 4/5, 6/7, 8/9, and 10/11. Stack the pages in order with the cover on top and all of the folds on the right side.

3. Staple the pages together along the left edge.

Connections to the Standards

Connections to the NCTM Math Standards

The activities in this book are designed to support you in meeting the following K–1 standards—including process standards, such as problem solving, reasoning and proof, and communication—recommended by the National Council of Teachers of Mathematics (NCTM):

Numbers and Operations

◆ Understand numbers, ways of representing numbers, relationships among numbers, and number systems

◆ Count with understanding and recognize "how many" in sets of objects

◆ Develop understanding of the relative position and magnitude of whole numbers and of ordinal and cardinal numbers and their connections

◆ Connect numerals to the quantities they represent

◆ Understand the effects of adding and subtracting whole numbers

◆ Use a variety of methods and tools to compute, including objects, mental computation, and paper and pencil

Algebra

◆ Understands patterns, relations, and functions
  • recognize, describe, and extend patterns
  • analyze how repeating patterns are generated

Geometry

◆ Analyze characteristics and properties of geometric shapes
  • recognize, name, compare, and sort shapes
  • describe attributes and parts of shapes

◆ Use visualization, spatial reasoning, and geometric modeling to solve problems
  • recognize and represent shapes from different perspectives

Measurement

◆ Understand measurable attributes of objects and the units, systems, and processes of measurement

◆ Recognize the attributes of time

◆ Understand how to measure using standard units

National Council of Teachers of Mathematics. (2000). *Principles and Standards for School Mathematics*. Reston, VA: NCTM. www.nctm.org

Connections to the McREL Language Arts Standards

Mid-continent Research for Education and Learning (McREL), a nationally recognized nonprofit organization, has compiled and evaluated national and state standards—and proposed what teachers should provide for their K–1 students to grow proficient in reading. The activities in this book support the following standards:

Reading

Uses the general skills and strategies of the reading process including:

◆ Uses mental images and meaning clues based on pictures and print to aid in comprehension of text

◆ Uses basic elements of phonetic and structural analysis to decode unknown words

◆ Understands level-appropriate sight words and vocabulary

◆ Uses self-correction strategies

Kendall, J. S., & Marzano, R. J. (2004). *Content knowledge: A compendium of standards and benchmarks for K–12 education*. Aurora, CO: Mid-continent Research for Education and Learning. Online database: http://www.mcrel.org/standards-benchmarks/

Patty's Pets

Skill One-to-One Correspondence

Getting Started

Gather a supply of counters in two different colors and put each color in a separate basket. Invite children to take a handful of each color. Then have them pair each counter of one color with a counter of the other color. As children work, encourage them to count out "one" for each counter and color (for instance, one blue, one red). If they have extra counters of one color, have children return the counters to the basket.

Completing the Mini-Book

Ask children to write their name on the cover, then cut out and glue the patterns onto the pages, as shown. Finally, have them complete the activity on the last page.

Reproducible Pages
mini-book: pages 8–13
patterns: page 14

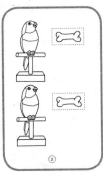

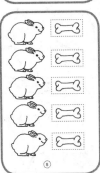

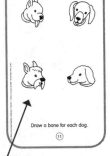

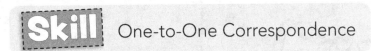

Draw a bone for each dog.

Taking It Further

Hold a stuffed "pet" party. Ask children to bring in a stuffed animal. Set out party hats, balloons, napkins, and other party supplies, making sure there are enough for each pet to have one of each item. Then invite children to take one of each kind of party item for their pet. Finally, serve one individually wrapped snack to each child to share with his or her pet. (Check for food allergies first.)

"We're hungry!" cried the pets.

"I'll feed everyone," Dog said.

Dog gave each bird a dog bone.

One for each.

"Yuck!" said the birds.

1

Cut & Paste Mini-Books: Math © 2010 by Nancy I. Sanders, Scholastic Teaching Resources (page 8)

Patty's Pets

by _____

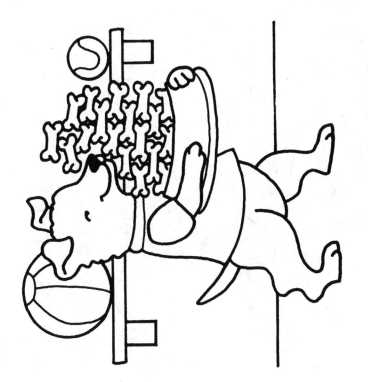

Dog gave each turtle a dog bone.

One for each.

"Yuck!" said the turtles.

③

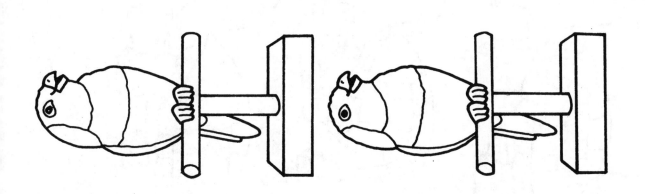

②

Dog gave each cat a dog bone.

One for each.

"Yuck!" said the cats.

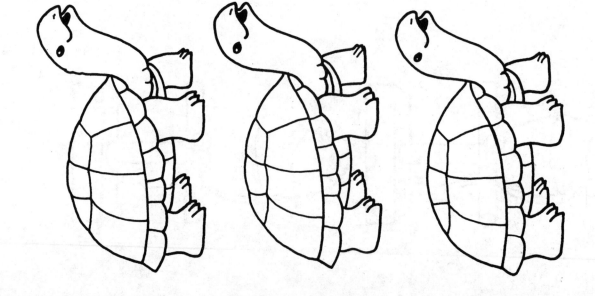

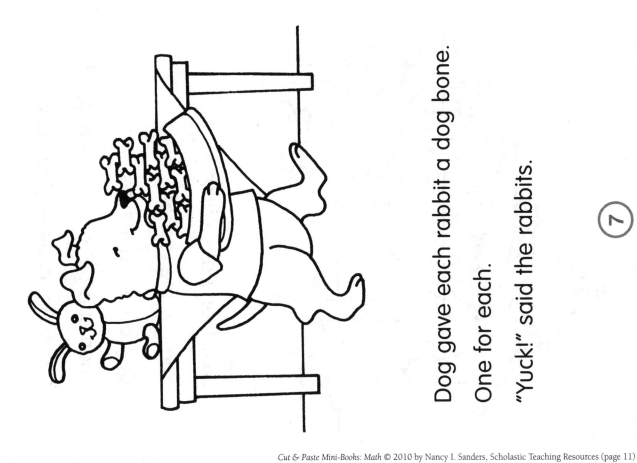

Dog gave each rabbit a dog bone.

One for each.

"Yuck!" said the rabbits.

7

6

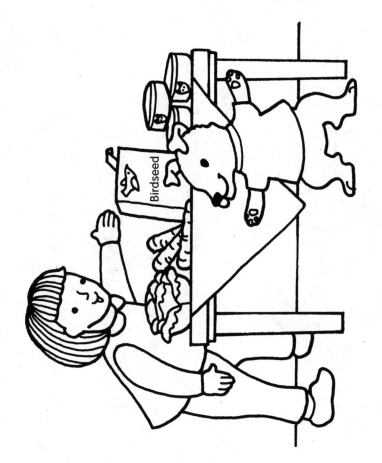

Just then Patty came in.

She put the rest of the dog bones in the bag.

Then she got out the right food.

"Yummy!" cheered the pets.

⑨

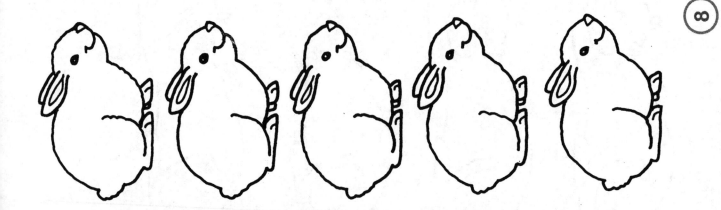

⑧

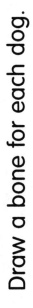

Draw a bone for each dog.

(11)

Cut & Paste Mini-Books: Math © 2010 by Nancy I. Sanders, Scholastic Teaching Resources (page 13)

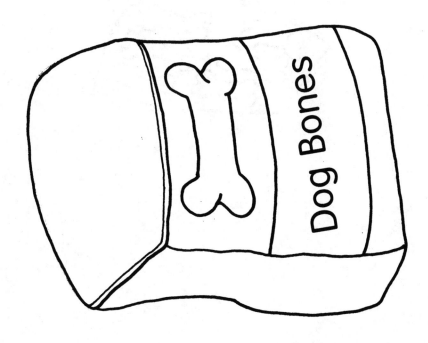

Dog Bones

Patty's Pets

Cut & Paste Patterns

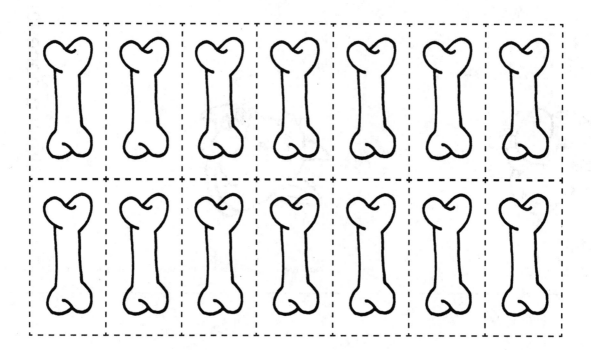

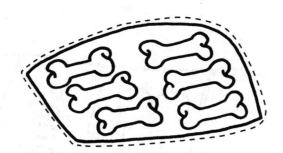

I Spy a Penguin

Getting Started

For this activity, you'll need white paper lunch bags and black and orange construction paper. First, invite children to make a penguin puppet by cutting out an orange beak and black wings and eyes to glue onto a bag. When finished, use the puppets to play counting games. For instance, ask children to put their puppet on their hand and go stand in one of several areas of the room that you've designated for this activity. Then have the children count the number of penguins that have gathered in each area. You might also ask some children to have their penguins "nap" while others "play." Have children count the number of penguins in each group.

Completing the Mini-Book

Ask children to write their name on the cover, then cut out and glue the patterns onto the pages, as shown. Finally, have them complete the activity on the last page.

Reproducible Pages
mini-book: pages 16–21
patterns: pages 22–23

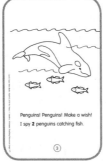

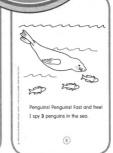

Penguins! Penguins! Young and old! I spy **1** penguin where it's cold. ①

②

Penguins! Penguins! Make a wish! I spy **2** penguins catching fish. ③

④

Penguins! Penguins! Fast and free! I spy **3** penguins in the sea. ⑤

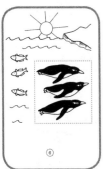

Penguins! Penguins! On the go! I spy **4** penguins in the snow. ⑥

⑦

⑧

Penguins! Penguins! In the night! I spy **5** penguins sleeping tight. ⑨

⑩

How many penguins are on the hill? _____
How many penguins are in the water? _____ ⑪

Count the penguins and write the answer.

Taking It Further

Make a word wall that features words children learn as they study penguins. Include key words from the story such as *young*, *old*, *cold*, *fish*, *fast*, *sea*, *snow*, *black*, and *white*. As the word wall grows, invite children to practice counting the number of words on the wall and the number of letters in the words.

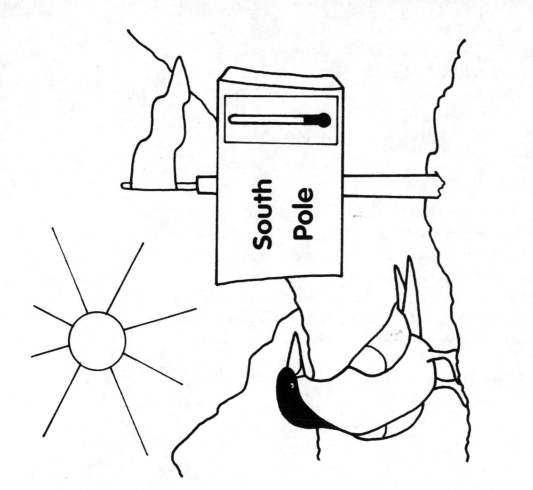

South Pole

Penguins! Penguins! Young and old!

I spy **1** penguin where it's cold.

Cut & Paste Mini-Books: Math © 2010 by Nancy I. Sanders, Scholastic Teaching Resources (page 16)

I Spy a Penguin

by _____

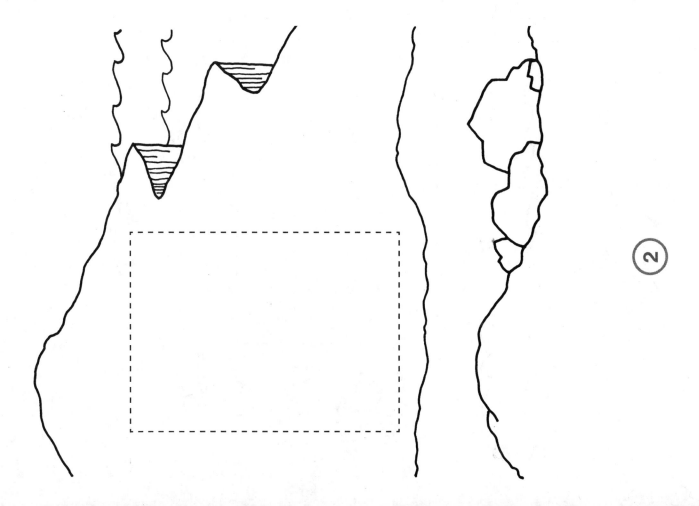

Penguins! Penguins! Make a wish!

I spy 2 penguins catching fish.

Penguins! Penguins! Fast and free!

I spy **3** penguins in the sea.

⑤

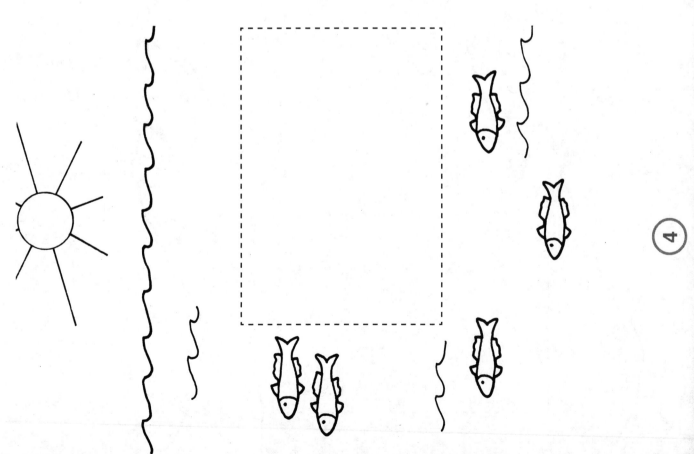

④

Penguins! Penguins! On the go!

I spy **4** penguins in the snow.

⑦

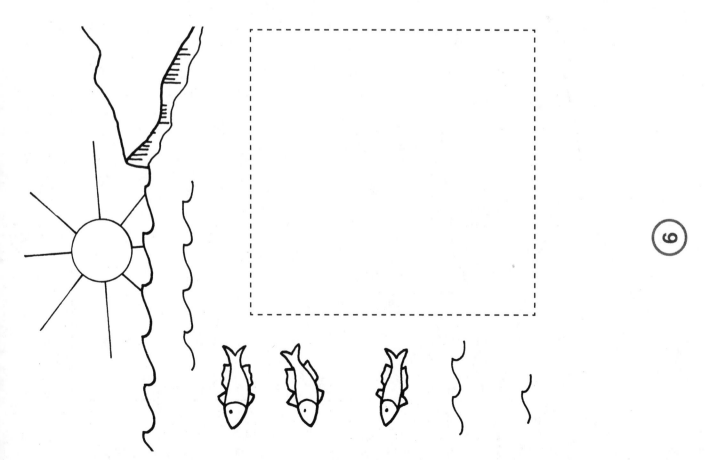

⑥

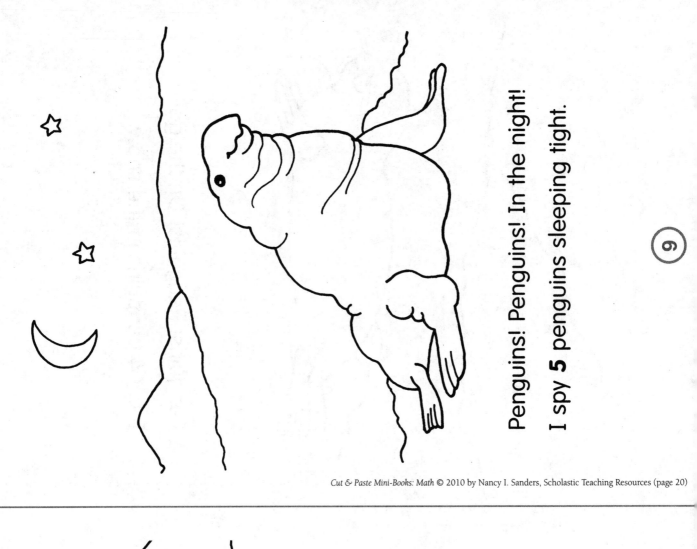

Penguins! Penguins! In the night!

I spy **5** penguins sleeping tight.

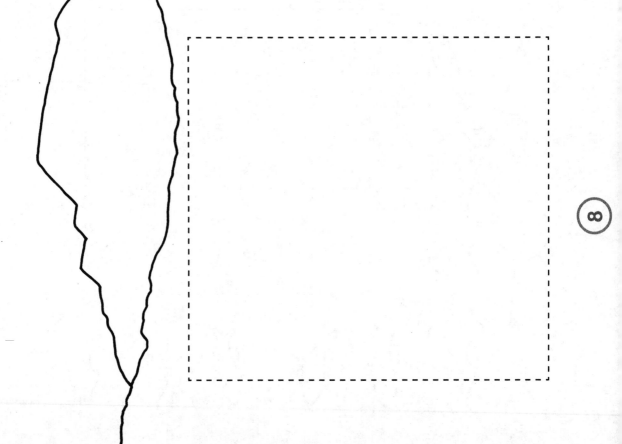

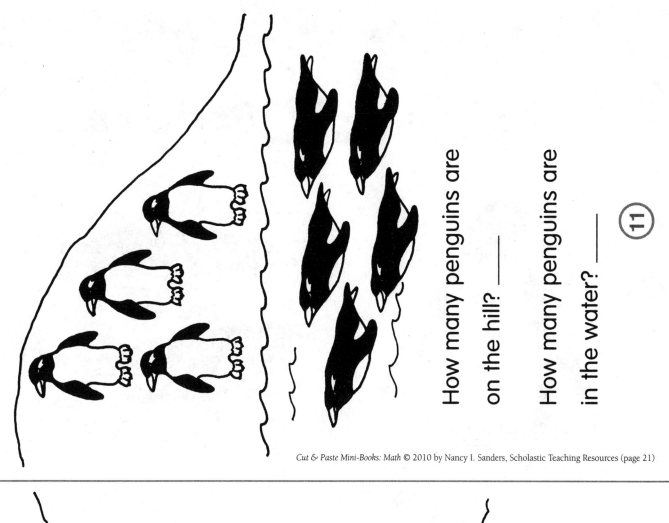

How many penguins are on the hill? ____

How many penguins are in the water? ____

11

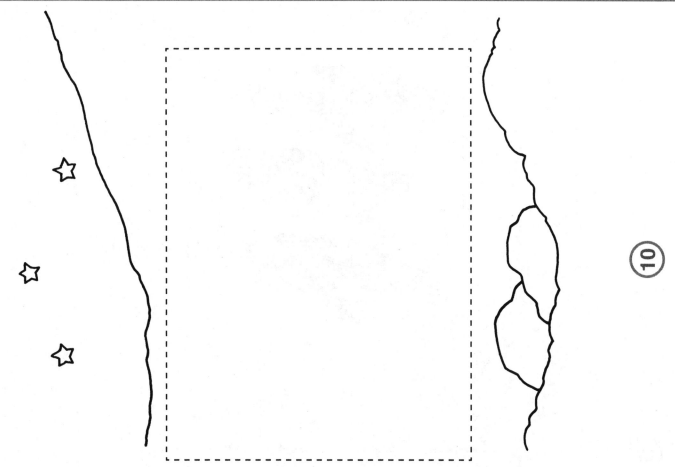

10

I Spy a Penguin

Cut & Paste Patterns

I Spy a Penguin

Cut & Paste Patterns

Fish, Fish, Fish

Getting Started

Ask children to imagine they are fish swimming in a lake (the classroom). Invite one volunteer to "swim" to the front of the room. In unison, count the number of fish in this part of the lake. Invite a second child to join the first fish. How many fish are now in this part of the lake? Have one child at a time join the group of fish, each time counting the number of fish in the group. When 10 fish are in this group, ask these children to swim back out into the lake. Then repeat the activity, gathering the fish in a different part of the lake and practicing counting up from 1 to 10.

Completing the Mini-Book

Ask children to write their name on the cover, then cut out and glue the patterns onto the pages, as shown. Finally, have them complete the activity on the last page.

Reproducible Pages
mini-book:
pages 25–30
patterns:
pages 31–32

    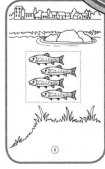 

  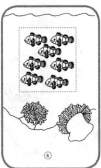  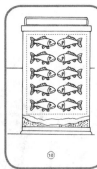 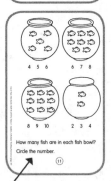

Count the fish and circle the number.

Taking It Further

At snack time, give each child a paper cup containing goldfish crackers. First, have them remove and count one goldfish before eating it. Then have them count two, three, and so on, until they run out of crackers. You can give all children the same number of goldfish to reach the same conclusions, or give them different amounts and have them compare their results.

3 fish are in a tank
swimming 'round and 'round.

(1)

Cut & Paste Mini-Books: Math © 2010 by Nancy I. Sanders, Scholastic Teaching Resources (page 25)

Fish, Fish, Fish

by _____

4 fish are in a river
just outside of town.

③

Cut & Paste Mini-Books: Math © 2010 by Nancy I. Sanders, Scholastic Teaching Resources (page 26)

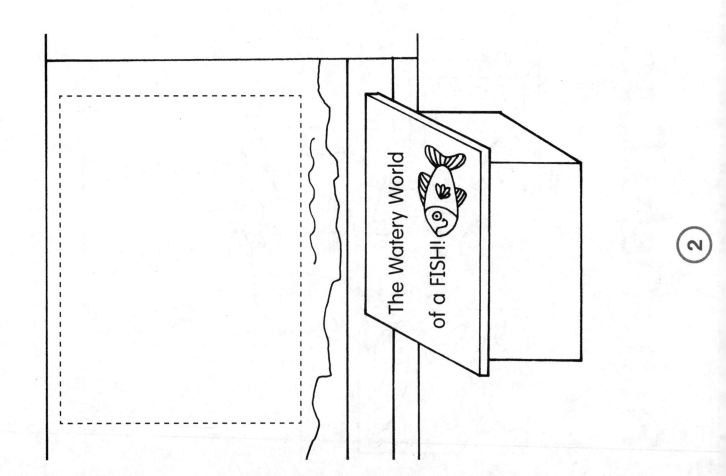

The Watery World
of a FISH!

②

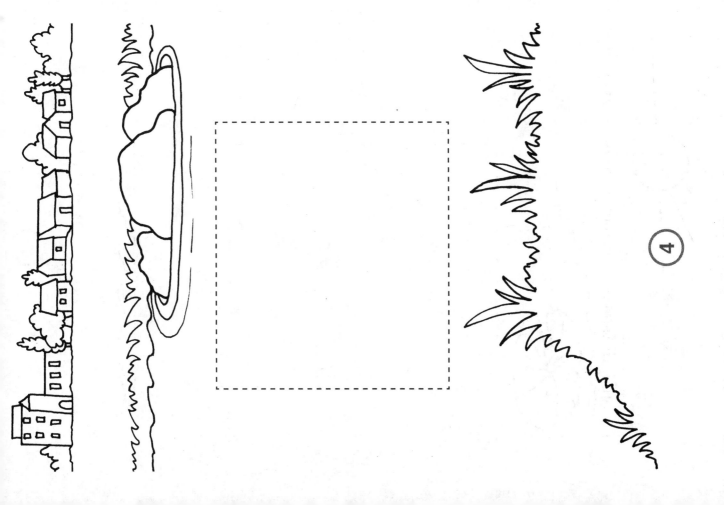

6 fish are in a pond swimming in the sun.

⑤

④

7 fish are in the ocean
having so much fun.

Cut & Paste Mini-Books: Math © 2010 by Nancy I. Sanders, Scholastic Teaching Resources (page 28)

7

6

10 fish are in a fish store.

I watch them swim and play.

I want to take them home with me.

I'm buying them today!

⑨

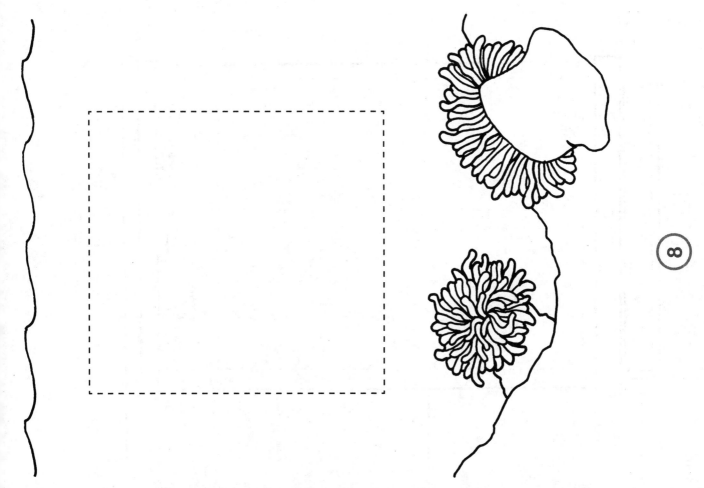

⑧

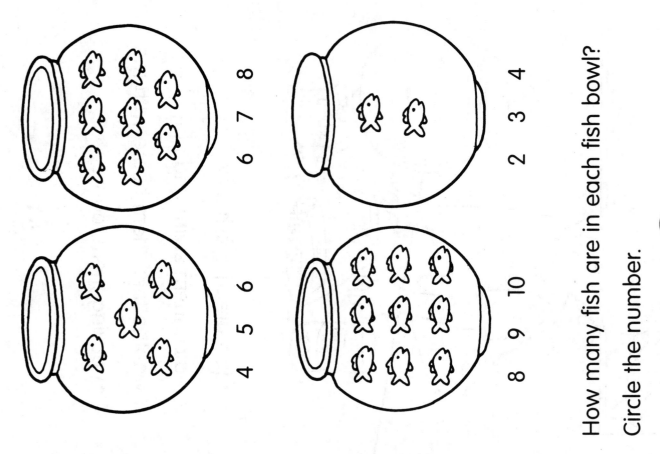

6 7 8

2 3 4

4 5 6

8 9 10

How many fish are in each fish bowl?

Circle the number.

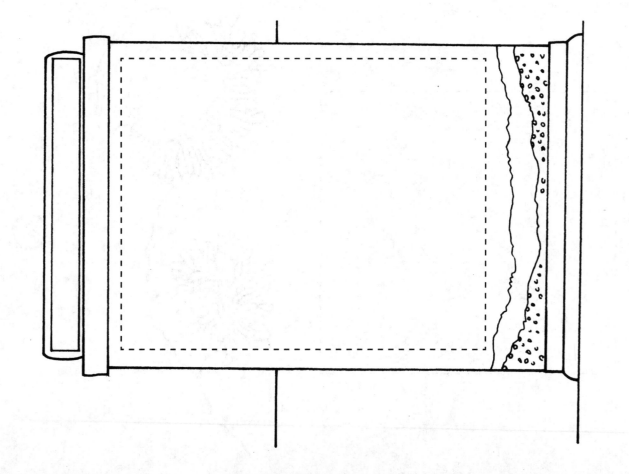

Fish, Fish, Fish

Cut & Paste Patterns

Fish, Fish, Fish

Cut & Paste Patterns

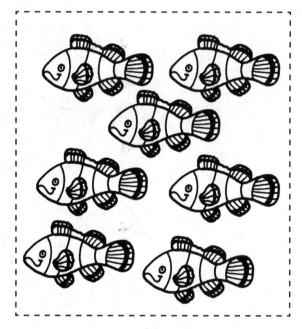

Fun With Pencils

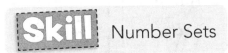

Skill Number Sets

Getting Started

Give children 12 counters each and have them divide their counters into two equal sets. How many counters are in each set? (*six*) Ask children to add the sets together to find out how many counters they have all together. Then show them how to write an addition sentence to represent the problem: 6 + 6 = 12. Next, have children divide their counters into three, then four, and finally six equal sets. Each time, model writing an addition sentence to show the total number of counters.

Completing the Mini-Book

Ask children to write their name on the cover, then cut out and glue the patterns onto the pages, as shown. Finally, have them complete the activity on the last page.

Reproducible Pages
mini-book:
pages 34–39
patterns:
page 40

Fun With Pencils

by _____

My teacher has **6** pencils.
They are all brand new.
She keeps them in a tray,
in three sets of **2**.
①

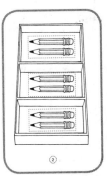
②

My cousins have **8** pencils.
They don't need any more.
They keep them in pouches,
in two sets of **4**.
③

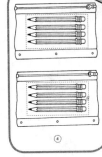
④

My best friend has **9** pencils.
He wants us all to see.
He keeps them in a backpack,
in three sets of **3**.
⑤

⑥

My father has **10** pencils.
He uses them to write.
He keeps them in cans,
in two sets of **5**.
⑦

⑧

Look! I have **12** pencils.
I'm as happy as can be.
I keep them in pencil boxes,
in four sets of **3**.
⑨

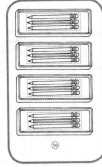
⑩

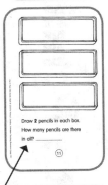

Draw **2** pencils in each box.
How many pencils are there
in all? _____
⑪

**Draw two pencils in each box.
Write the total number of pencils.**

Taking It Further

Pair up children and give each pair several tall paper cups and an assortment of pencils. Ask the partners to make two equal sets of pencils and put each set in a separate cup. How many pencils are in each cup? How many pencils are there in all? Have children write an addition sentence to show their answer. Repeat the activity, this time having children create three equal sets of pencils to put in three cups, then four equal sets to put in four cups, and so on.

Good Morning

My teacher has **6** pencils.

They are all brand new.

She keeps them in a tray,

in three sets of **2**.

Cut & Paste Mini-Books: Math © 2010 by Nancy I. Sanders, Scholastic Teaching Resources (page 34)

Fun With Pencils

by _____

My cousins have **8** pencils.

They don't need any more.

They keep them in pouches,

in two sets of **4**.

3

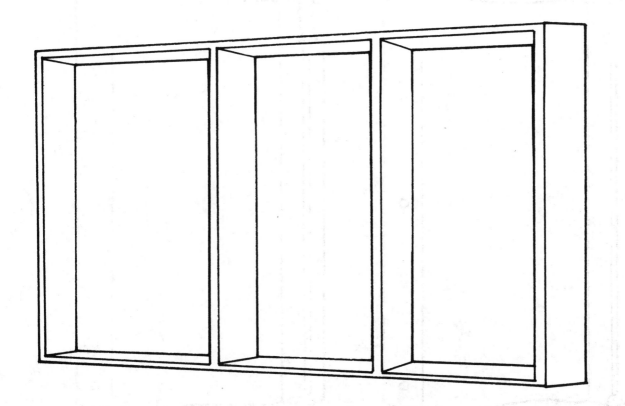

2

My best friend has **9** pencils.

He wants us all to see.

He keeps them in a backpack,

in three sets of **3**.

5

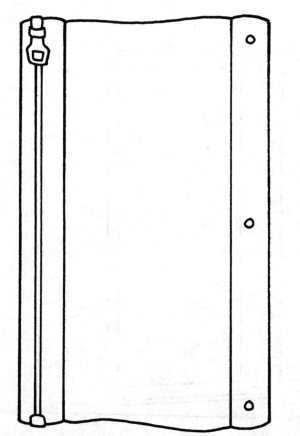

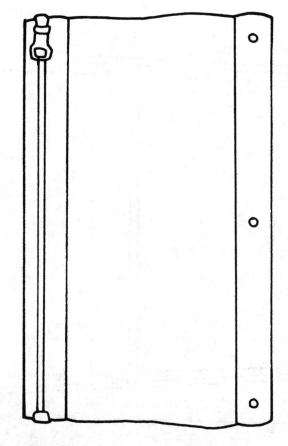

4

My father has **10** pencils.

He uses them to write.

He keeps them in cans,

in two sets of **5**.

(7)

Cut & Paste Mini-Books: Math © 2010 by Nancy I. Sanders, Scholastic Teaching Resources (page 37)

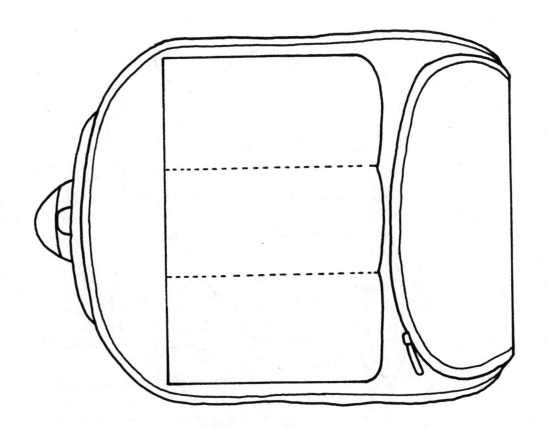

(6)

Look! I have **12** pencils.

I'm as happy as can be.

I keep them in pencil boxes,

in four sets of **3**.

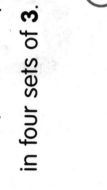

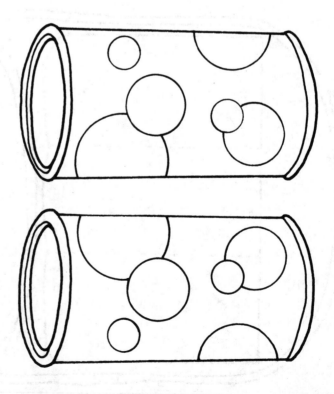

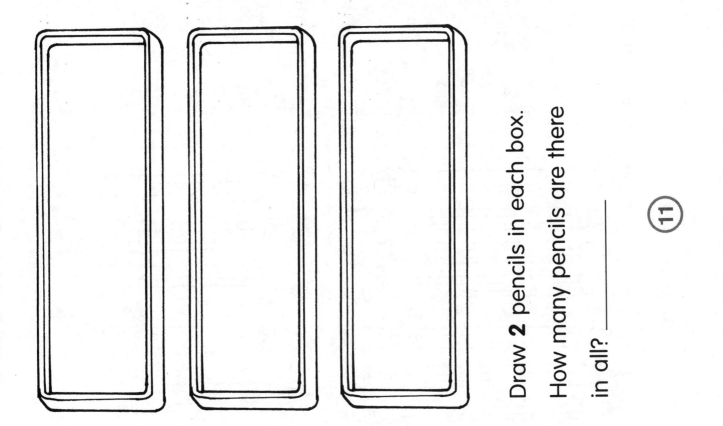

Draw **2** pencils in each box.

How many pencils are there in all? _____

11

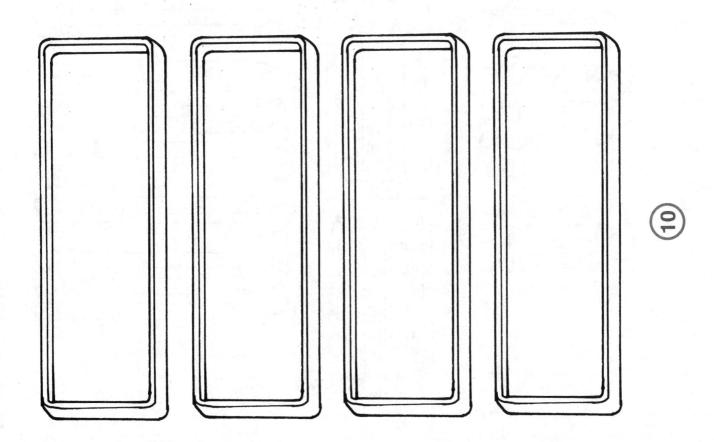

10

Fun With Pencils

Cut & Paste Patterns

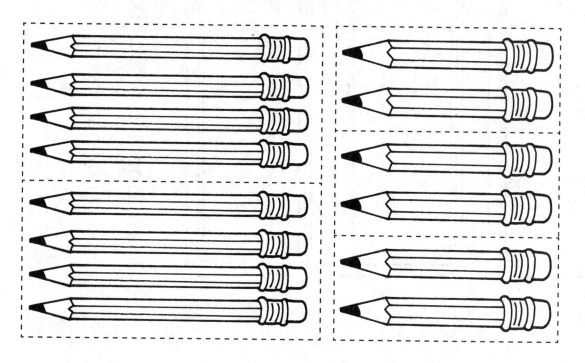

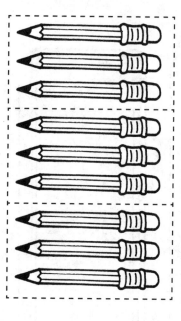

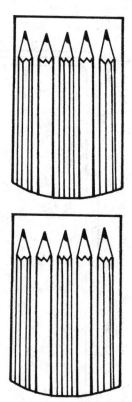

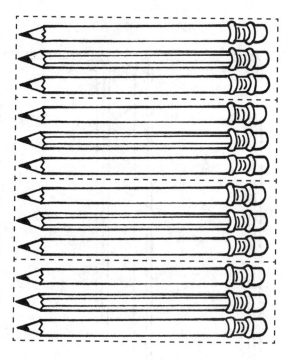

I Like Shoes!

Getting Started

Write the numbers 1 through 12 on the chalkboard. Together with the class, practice counting aloud from 1 to 12, pointing to the numbers as you go. Next have children count from 1 to 12, saying the even numbers louder than the odd numbers. Then discuss the number pattern. Finally, have children skip-count by twos from 1 to 12, pointing to only the even numbers as they count. Later, you might have them practice skip counting by twos up to 20, then 30.

Completing the Mini-Book

Ask children to write their name on the cover, then cut out and glue the patterns onto the pages, as shown. Finally, have them complete the activity on the last page.

Reproducible Pages
mini-book: pages 42–47
patterns: page 48

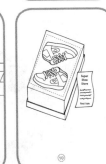
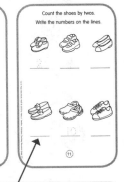

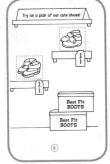

Count the shoes by twos and write the numbers.

Taking It Further

Assemble children into groups of two to six children. Then have the groups line up and count their shoes by twos. How many shoes are in each group? To extend children's skip-counting skills, have them count the number of eyes or ears in each group by twos. For additional skip-counting fun, children might also try counting their fingers (or toes) by fives.

Shoes are on a rug

pretty as can be.

I count 10 shoes

for my friends and me.

2, 4, 6, 8, 10.

(1)

I Like Shoes!

by _____

Here in my room
over by the door,
I count 8 shoes
sitting on the floor.
2, 4, 6, 8.

③

②

I take a little swim

where it's nice and cool.

I count 6 shoes

lined up by the pool.

2, 4, 6.

⑤

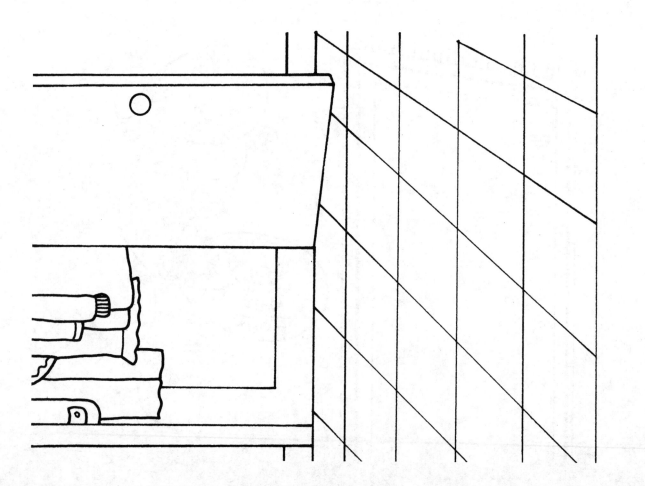

④

I go with my dad
to shop at the mall.
I count 4 shoes
sitting by the wall.

2, 4.

⑦

⑥

My new pair of shoes

are in the shoe box.

I count 2 shoes

I like them lots and lots!

2!

⑨

Try on a pair of our cute shoes!

SALE

SALE

Best Fit BOOTS

Best Fit BOOTS

⑧

Count the shoes by twos.

Write the numbers on the lines.

_____

2

_____

_____

_____

11

Cut & Paste Mini-Books: Math © 2010 by Nancy I. Sanders, Scholastic Teaching Resources (page 47)

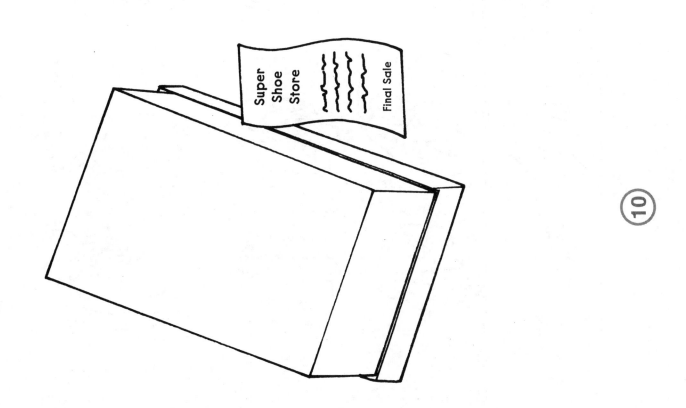

Super
Shoe
Store

Final Sale

10

I Like Shoes!

Cut & Paste Patterns

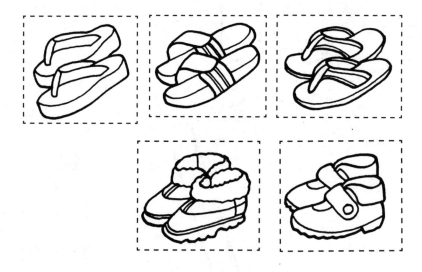

Borp's Trip

Getting Started

Work with children to list the steps to follow when doing activities such as baking a cake, planting a seed, or wrapping a gift. Write each step for the specified activity on separate index cards and mix up the cards. Then invite children to put the cards in order and use them to tell the sequence of steps for that activity. Point out how using ordinal numbers is helpful in sequencing the steps (for example: *first*, cut a piece of wrapping paper to fit around the gift; *second*, place the gift in the center of the paper; and so on).

Completing the Mini-Book

Ask children to write their name on the cover, then cut out and glue the patterns onto the pages, as shown. Finally, have them complete the activity on the last page.

Reproducible Pages
mini-book:
pages 50–55

patterns:
page 56

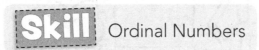

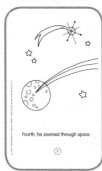
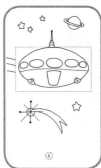

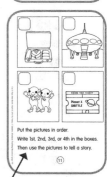

Write 1ˢᵗ, 2ⁿᵈ, 3ʳᵈ, or 4ᵗʰ to put the pictures in order.

Taking It Further

Write ordinal numbers on the back of the cards from "Getting Started" (above) to indicate the correct order of the cards for each activity. Place each card set into a zippered plastic bag labeled with the activity. Also, create a set of sequencing cards for *Borp's Trip*. Place all of the bags into a small suitcase. Then invite partners to work together to sequence the cards for each activity. Children can check the back of the cards to see if they put them in the correct order.

49

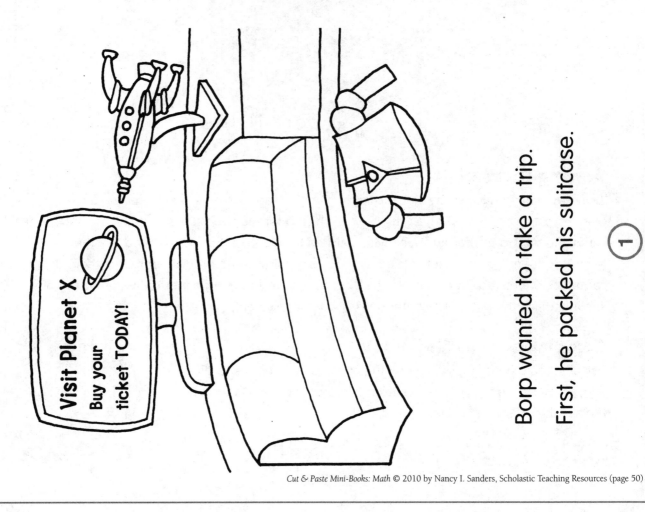

Visit Planet X

Visit Planet X
Buy your
ticket TODAY!

Borp wanted to take a trip.

First, he packed his suitcase.

1

Borp's Trip

by _____

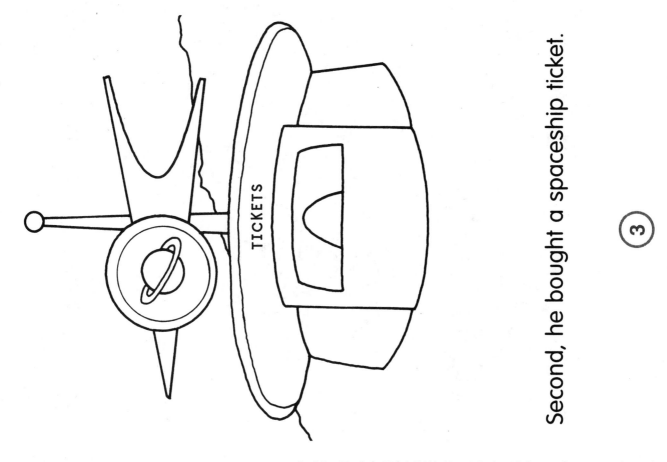

Second, he bought a spaceship ticket.

③

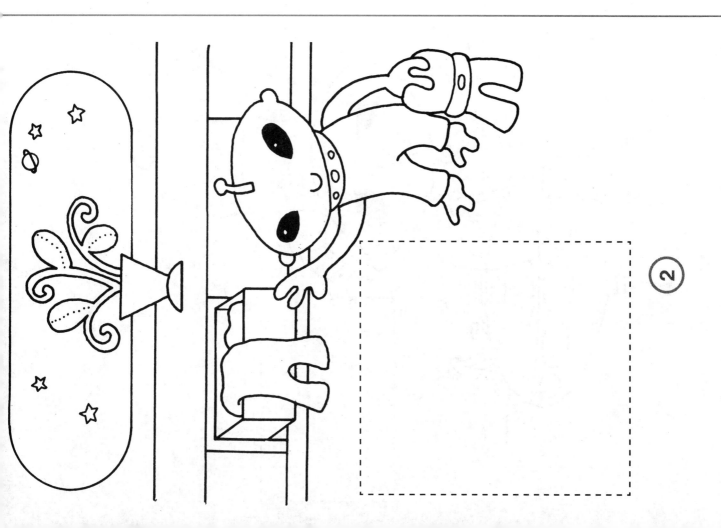

②

Third, he got in the spaceship.

⑤

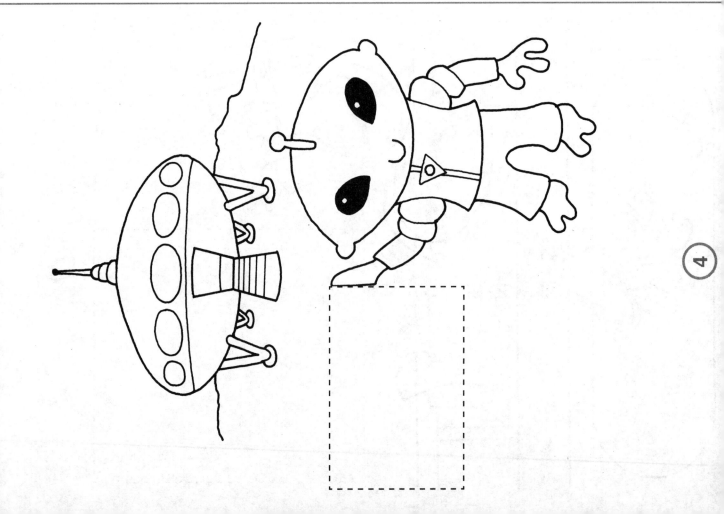

④

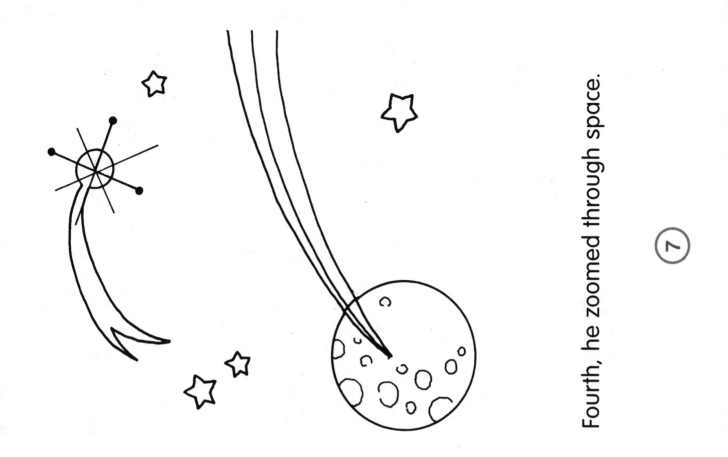

Fourth, he zoomed through space.

Cut & Paste Mini-Books: Math © 2010 by Nancy I. Sanders, Scholastic Teaching Resources (page 53)

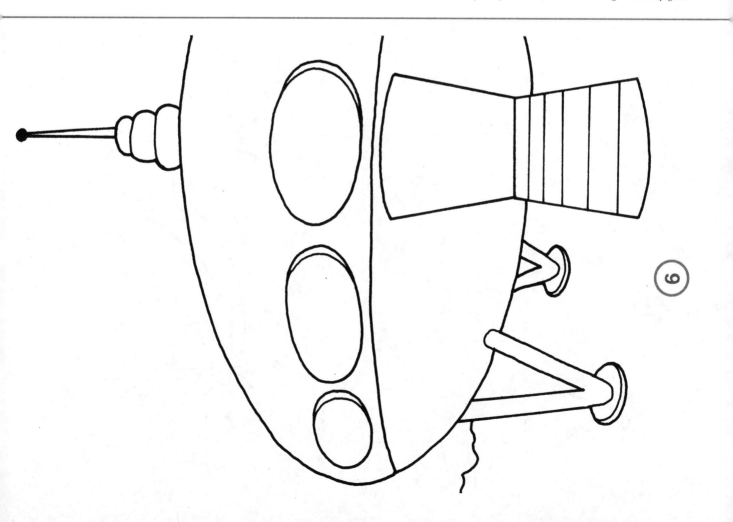

Fifth, he landed on a planet far away.

Finally, Borp was with his friends!

What a fun trip!

⑨

⑧

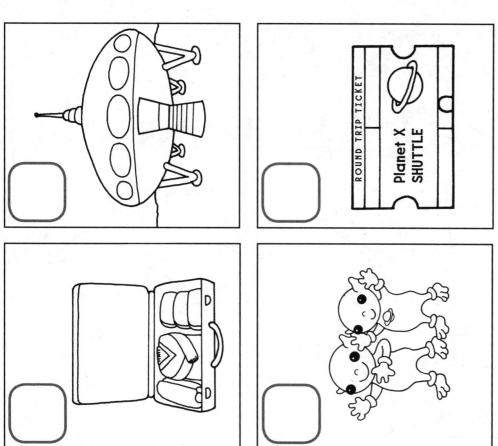

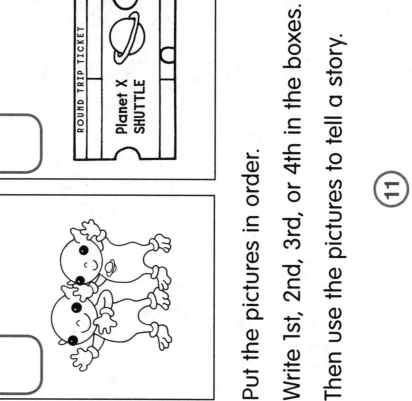

ROUND TRIP TICKET

Planet X
SHUTTLE

Put the pictures in order.

Write 1st, 2nd, 3rd, or 4th in the boxes.

Then use the pictures to tell a story.

⑪

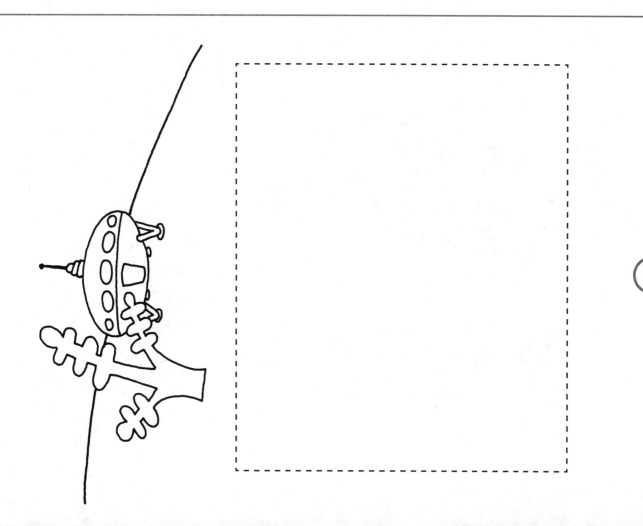

⑩

Borp's Trip

Cut & Paste Patterns

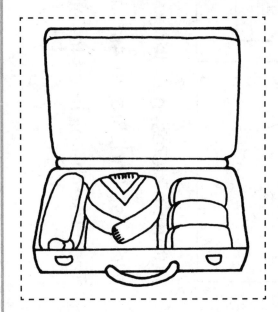

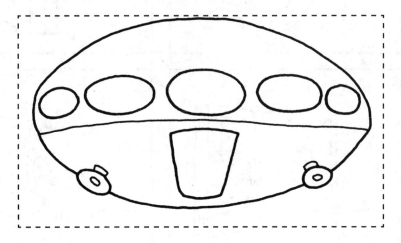

ROUND TRIP TICKET

Planet X
SHUTTLE

Shapes All Around

Skill Shapes

Getting Started

Cut out a large square, circle, triangle, oval, and rectangle from sturdy poster board. Then cut out several 3-inch shapes from construction paper to match each large shape. Distribute the smaller shapes to children. Next, hold up a large shape and point out its attributes and unique characteristics. Ask children to identity the shape. Then invite those children who have a matching shape to clip it to the large shape with a clothespin. Repeat for each large shape.

Completing the Mini-Book

Ask children to write their name on the cover, then cut out and glue the patterns onto the pages, as shown. Finally, have them complete the activity on the last page.

Reproducible Pages
mini-book: pages 58–63
patterns: page 64

Draw an X on the shape that does not belong in each row.

Taking It Further

Title a poster "Shapes on My Face." Under the title, write "Today, my face has two ____ eyes, a ___ nose, and a ___ mouth." Leave each blank long and tall enough to fit a word card on it. Then label index cards with these shape names: *circle, square, oval, triangle,* and *rectangle.* Laminate the poster and word cards. Display the poster in a learning center and add paper plates, glue, and a supply of shape cutouts that correspond to the word cards. To use, tape a word card to each blank on the poster. Then have children create a paper-plate face to match the text.

Shapes are fun for everyone.

A circle!

A circle is lots of fun.

A circle is round
like the yellow sun.

Shapes All Around

by _____

A square!

A square has 4 sides alike.

A square is a shed

where we keep our bike.

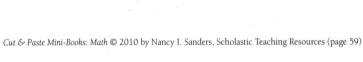

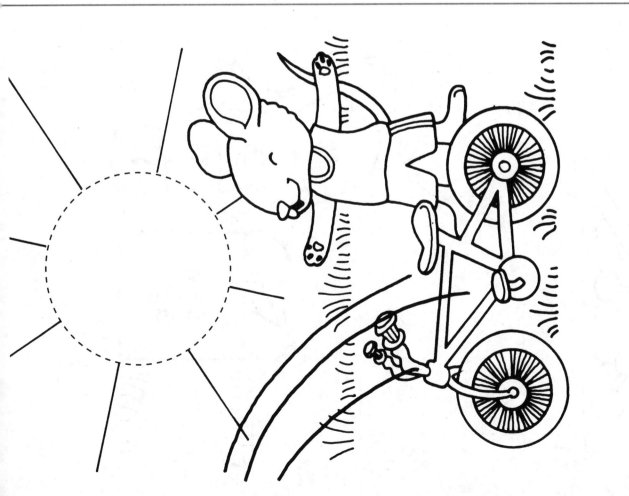

2

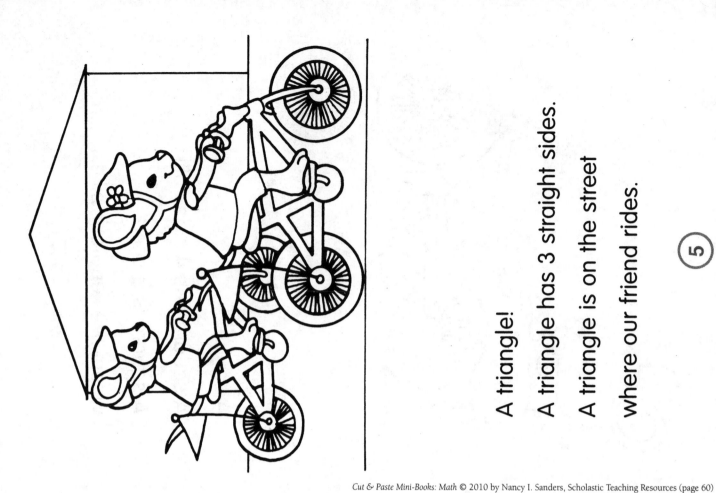

A triangle!

A triangle has 3 straight sides.

A triangle is on the street

where our friend rides.

Cut & Paste Mini-Books: Math © 2010 by Nancy I. Sanders, Scholastic Teaching Resources (page 60)

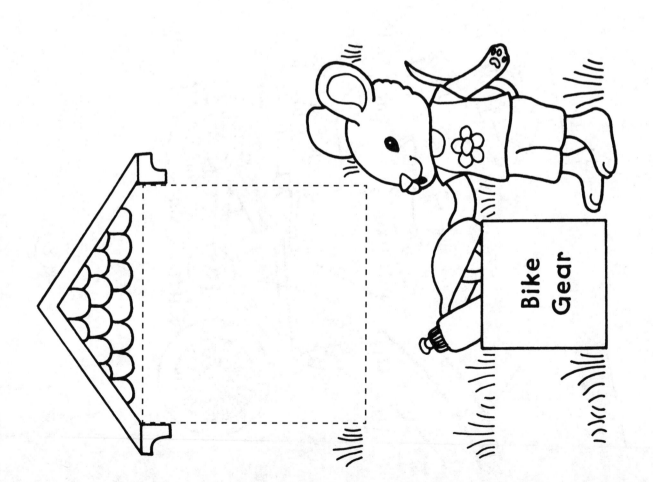

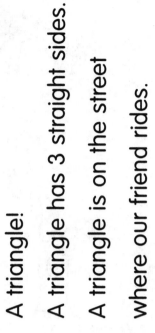

Bike
Gear

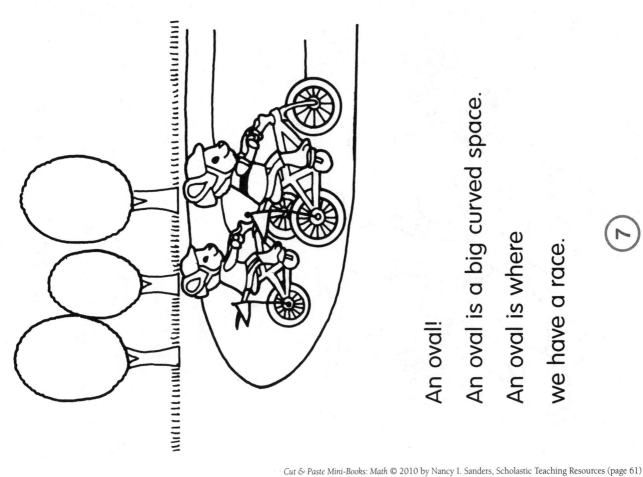

An oval!

An oval is a big curved space.

An oval is where

we have a race.

Cut & Paste Mini-Books: Math © 2010 by Nancy I. Sanders, Scholastic Teaching Resources (page 61)

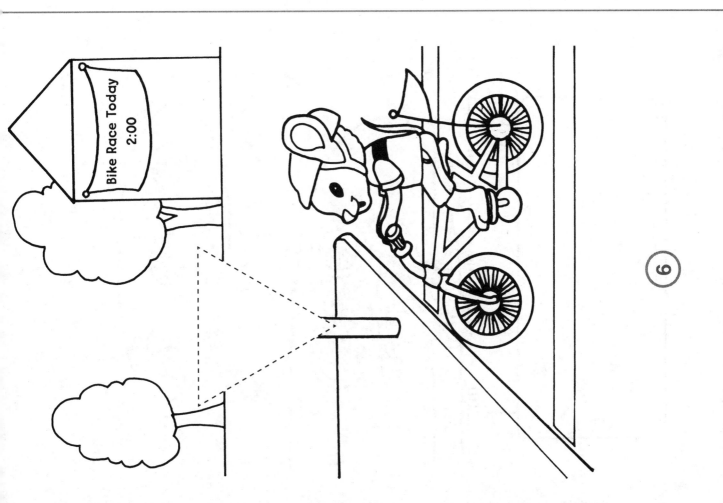

Bike Race Today
2:00

A rectangle!

A rectangle is a lot of fun.

A rectangle is a box

with a prize that is won.

Shapes are fun for everyone!

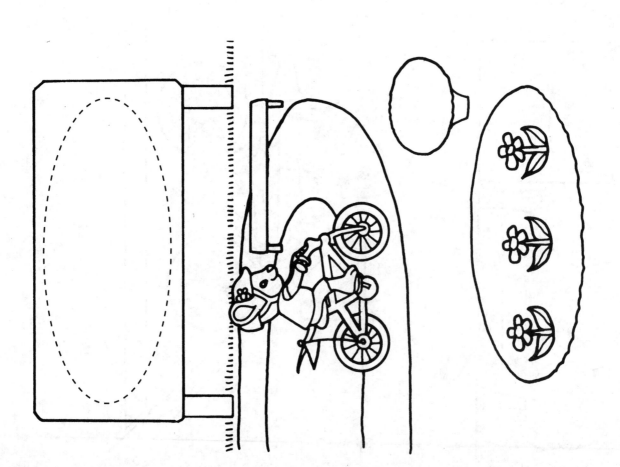

8

Draw an X on each shape
that does not belong.

circle	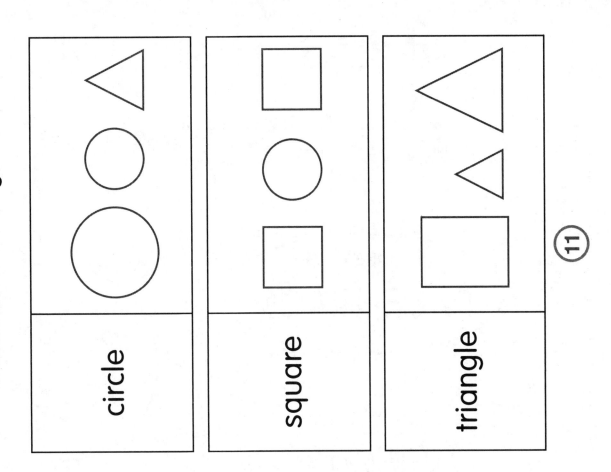
square	
triangle	

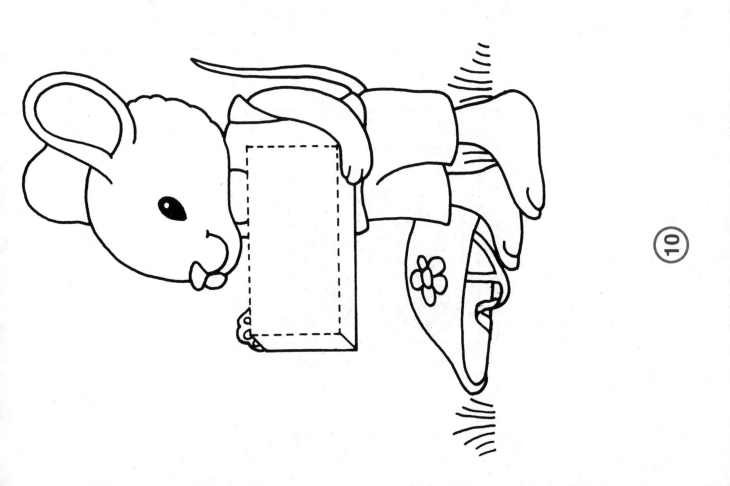

Shapes All Around

Cut & Paste Patterns

Mouseville
RACE TRACK

YIELD

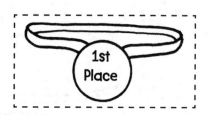

1st
Place

I See Patterns!

Getting Started

Introduce students to patterns with this fun patterning activity. First, list several noises that cars make, such as *honk, beep, toot,* and *rattle*. Then use a few of the sounds to create simple verbal patterns, for example: *honk, honk, beep, beep*. Ask children to repeat each pattern that you model. When children become comfortable repeating the patterns, challenge them to repeat, and then continue, the patterns after your demonstrations. You might also invite volunteers to make up new patterns for the class to continue.

Completing the Mini-Book

Ask children to write their name on the cover, then cut out and glue the patterns onto the pages, as shown. Finally, have them complete the activity on the last page.

> **Reproducible Pages**
> mini-book:
> pages 66–71
> patterns:
> page 72

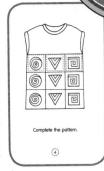

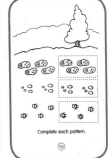
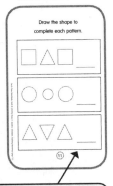

Draw the shape to complete each pattern.

Taking It Further

Seat groups of five children in a circle. Instruct one child in each group to use sounds made by animals to create a two- or three-sound pattern, such as *moo, woof, chirp, moo, woof, chirp*. Ask each child, in turn, to continue the pattern until every child has taken part. Then repeat the activity, starting with a different child. Encourage children to use animal sounds different from the ones previously used.

I see patterns on a quilt
that keeps me warm at night.

1

Cut & Paste Mini-Books: Math © 2010 by Nancy I. Sanders, Scholastic Teaching Resources (page 66)

I See Patterns!

by _____

I see patterns on a shirt
that is colorful and bright.

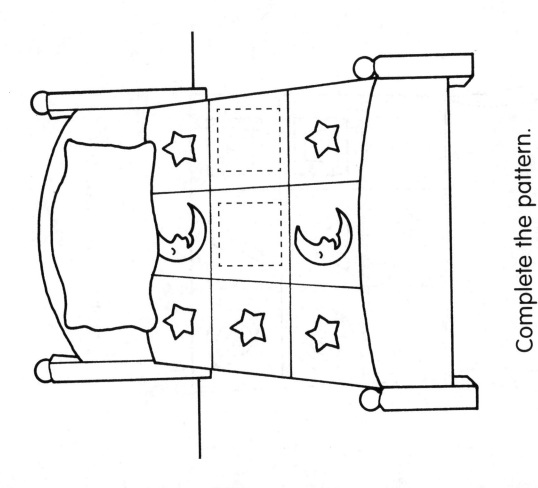

Complete the pattern.

②

I see patterns on a box
that has a gift inside.

⑤

Complete the pattern.

④

I see patterns on the board
that go from side to side.

Cut & Paste Mini-Books: Math © 2010 by Nancy I. Sanders, Scholastic Teaching Resources (page 69)

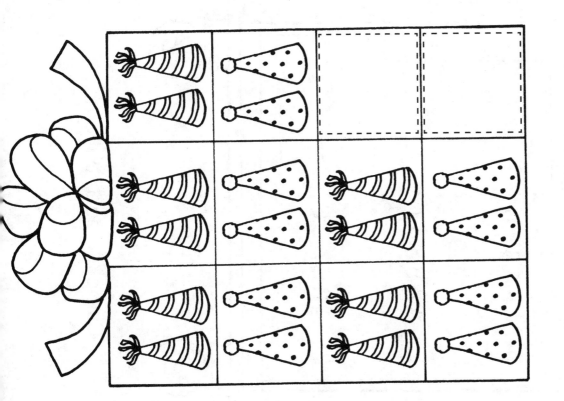

Complete the pattern.

6

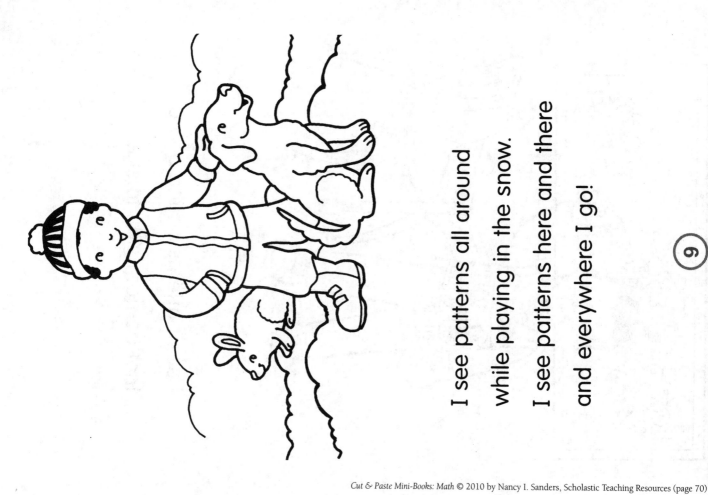

I see patterns all around while playing in the snow.

I see patterns here and there and everywhere I go!

⑨

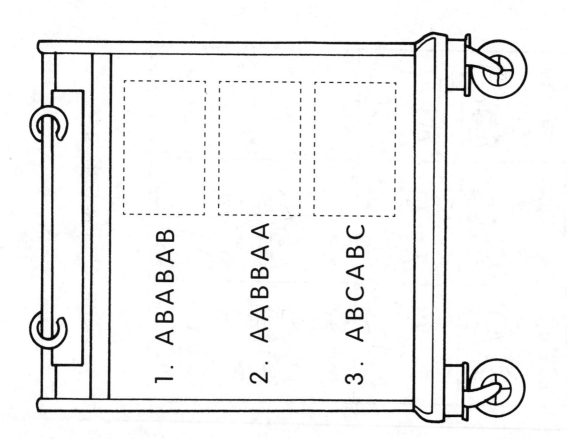

1. A B A B A B

2. A A B B A A

3. A B C A B C

Complete each pattern.

⑧

Draw the shape to
complete each pattern.

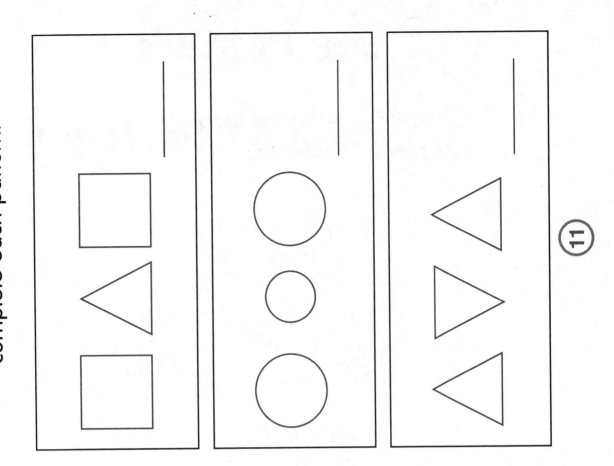

⓫

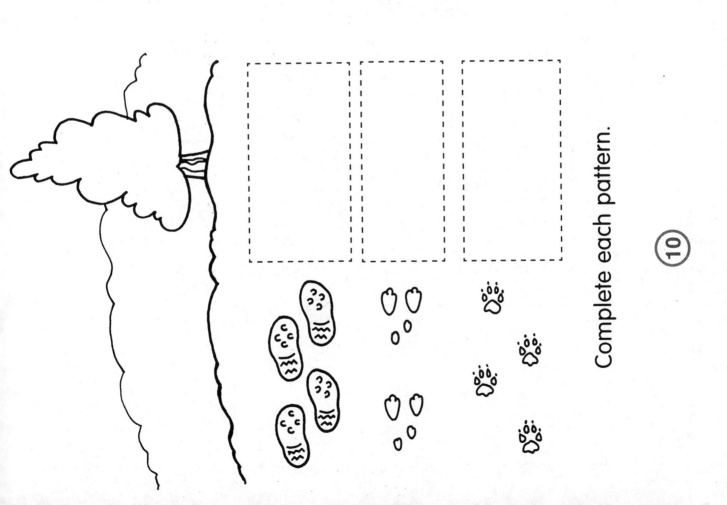

Complete each pattern.

❿

I See Patterns!

Cut & Paste Patterns

A B A B A B	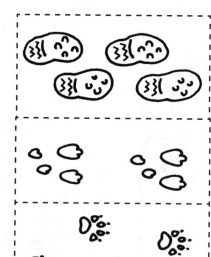
B B A A B B	
A B C A B C	

Flowers in My Basket

Skill Addition

Getting Started

Give children different quantities of counters from 1 to 10. Then ask them to form two sets using the counters. For example, have children use five counters to create a set of two and another set of three counters. After making the sets, explain that children can use the sets in an addition number sentence. Show them how to write the number sentence, such as 2 + 3 = 5. Repeat the activity as often as desired, having children use different quantities and set sizes to create addition number sentences with sums up to 10.

Completing the Mini-Book

Ask children to write their name on the cover, then cut out and glue the patterns onto the pages, as shown. Finally, have them complete the activity on the last page.

Reproducible Pages
mini-book: pages 74–79
patterns: page 80

Add the flowers and draw the total number of flowers in each basket. Write a number sentence.

Taking It Further

Invite children to cut out construction-paper flowers and glue each one to a craft stick, creating as many flowers as desired up to ten. Then give children an 8-ounce paper-cup "flowerpot" filled with dried beans. To practice addition, pair up children and have them "plant" a few flowers in their flowerpot. Then ask the partners to add their flowers to find out how many in all are in the pots. They might also write number sentences to show their addition problems.

73

I have some pretty baskets.

What should I put in them?

I'll add **1** flower to this one.

Now watch the fun begin!

(1)

Flowers in My Basket

by _____

1 flower in my basket
is so pretty to see.
I add **2** more flowers
and now I have _____.

$0 + 1 = $ _____

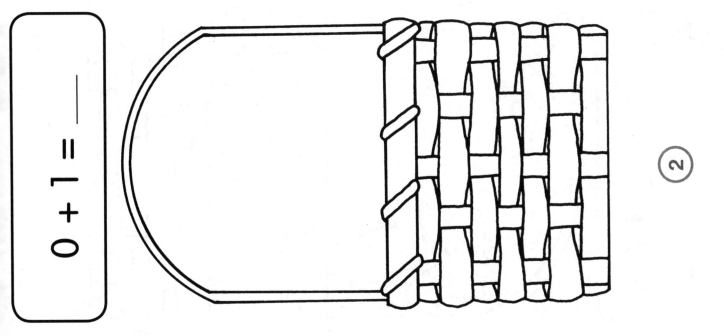

②

3 flowers in my basket
were from the grocery store.
I add **1** more flower
and now I have _____.

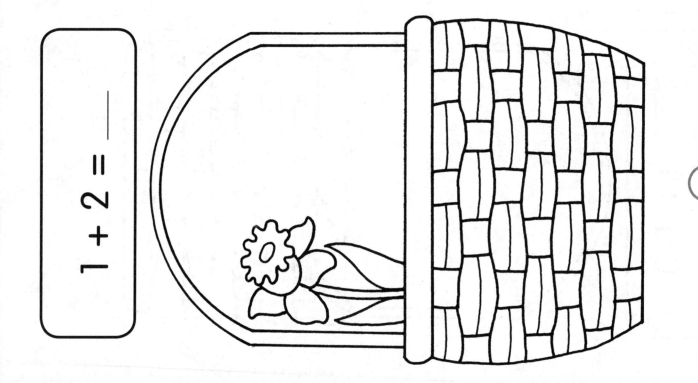

1 + 2 = _____

④

4 flowers in my basket
are standing tall and straight.
I add **4** more flowers
and now I have _____.

⑦

3 + 1 = _____

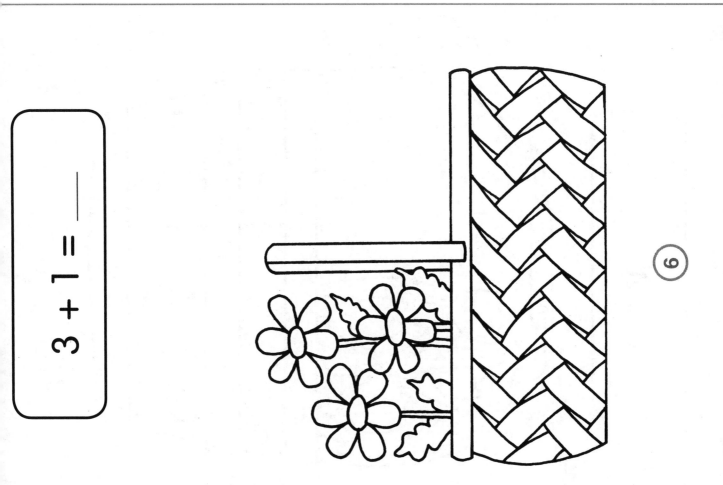

⑥

8 flowers in my basket

were a gift from my friend.

I add **2** more flowers.

Now I have _____!

⑨

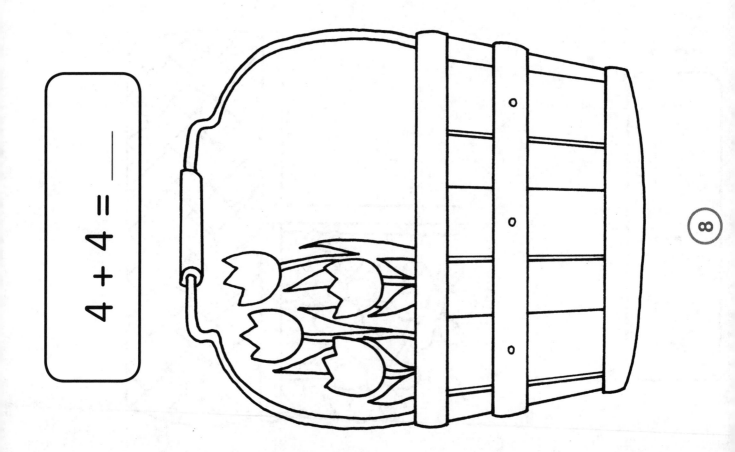

4 + 4 = _____

⑧

Add the flowers.

Then draw your answer.

Write a number sentence.

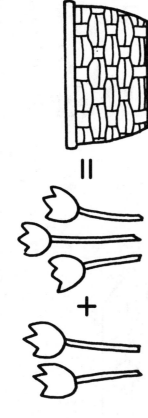

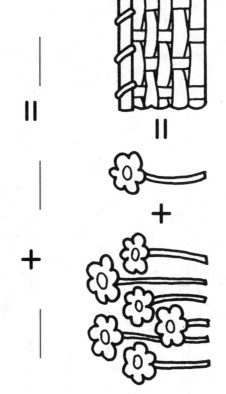

$$8 + 2 = \underline{\hspace{1cm}}$$

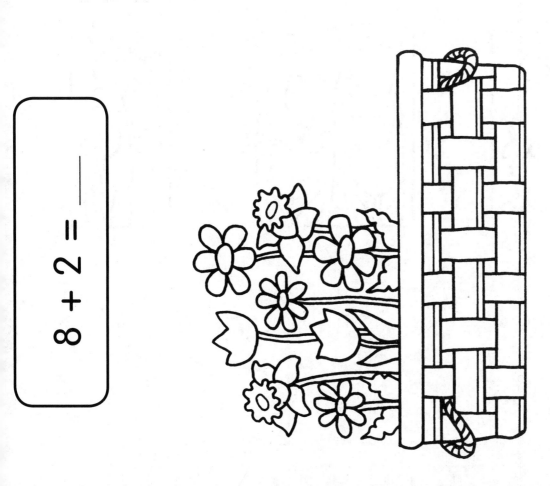

(11)

(10)

Flowers in My Basket

Cut & Paste Patterns

Jellybeans to Share

Skill Subtraction

Getting Started

Place ten teddy bear counters on a sheet of paper. Then make up a story about a few of the teddy bears leaving "home" to go somewhere else, such as school. Each time a group of teddy bears leaves, point out the number left at home. Write a subtraction number sentence to show what happened. Afterward, form small groups and give each group ten teddy bear counters and a sheet of paper. Ask children to make up their own teddy bear stories to share with the group. As children tell their stories, encourage the group to write subtraction problems to go with the story.

Completing the Mini-Book

Ask children to write their name on the cover, then cut out and glue the patterns onto the pages, as shown. Finally, have them complete the activity on the last page.

Reproducible Pages
mini-book:
pages 82–87
patterns:
page 88

Jellybeans to Share

by _____

I had **10** jellybeans in a curvy line. I ate **1** jellybean. Now I have _____

10 – 1 = ___ ①

②

I had **9** jellybeans on a pretty plate. I gave **1** to my brother. Now I have _____

9 – 1 = ___ ③

④

I had **8** jellybeans on the stump of a tree. I gave **5** to my grandma. Now I have _____

8 – 5 = ___ ⑤

⑥

I had **3** jellybeans in a dish under the sun. I shared **2** with my friends. Now I have _____

3 – 2 = ___ ⑦

⑧

I went with my mom to the candy store. I bought a bag of jellybeans. Now I have **10** more! ⑨

⑩

$\begin{array}{r} 5 \\ -2 \\ \hline \end{array}$ $\begin{array}{r} 7 \\ -3 \\ \hline \end{array}$

Trace the numbers. Write how many are left in each jar. ⑪

Trace the subtraction problems and write the answers.

Taking It Further

Whom would children share a bag of 10 jellybeans with and how many would they share with that person? After children respond, have them draw a picture of themselves sharing their jellybeans. Help them write "*I like to share jellybeans with _____*" on their page, filling in the person's name at the end of the sentence. Also, have children write a subtraction number sentence to go with their picture. Finally, bind the pictures into a class book titled, "Jellybeans Are Fun to Share!"

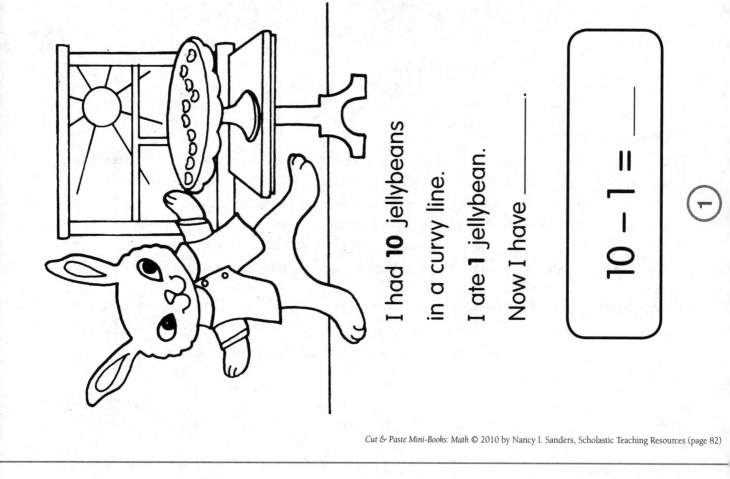

I had **10** jellybeans
in a curvy line.

I ate **1** jellybean.

Now I have _____.

10 – 1 = ____

①

Jellybeans to Share

by _____

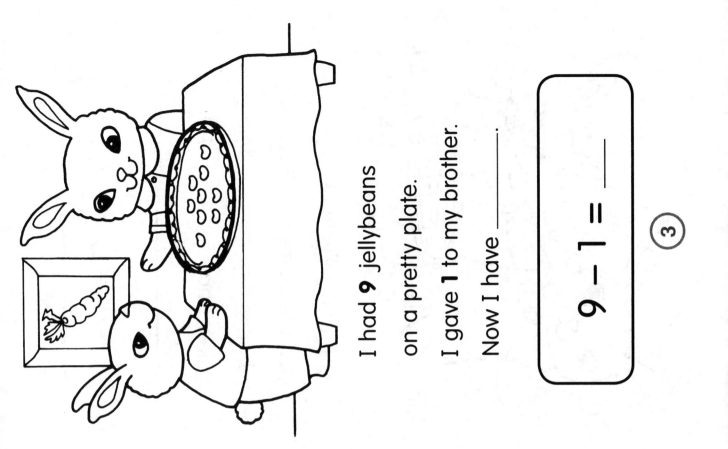

I had **9** jellybeans
on a pretty plate.

I gave **1** to my brother.

Now I have _____.

9 – 1 = ___

3

2

I had **8** jellybeans
on the stump of a tree.
I gave **5** to my grandma.
Now I have _____.

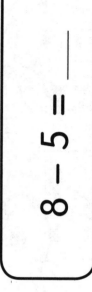

8 – 5 = ___

⑤

Cut & Paste Mini-Books: Math © 2010 by Nancy I. Sanders, Scholastic Teaching Resources (page 84)

④

I had **3** jellybeans
in a dish under the sun.
I shared **2** with my friends.
Now I have _____.

3 − 2 = ____

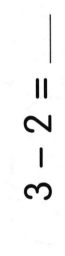

I went with my mom
to the candy store.
I bought a bag of
jellybeans.
Now I have **10** more!

⑧

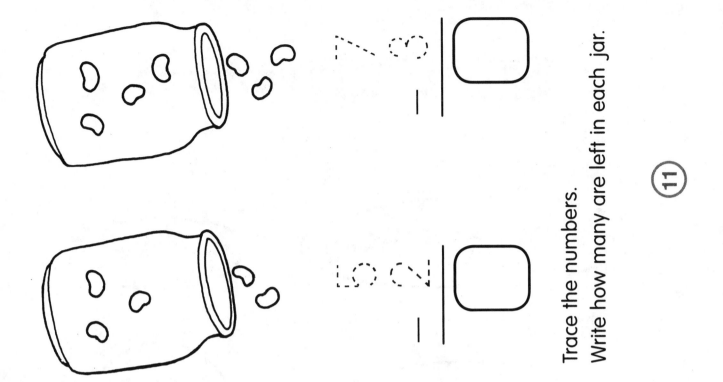

Trace the numbers.
Write how many are left in each jar.

7 3 — 1

5 2 — 1

11

10

Jellybeans to Share

Cut & Paste Patterns

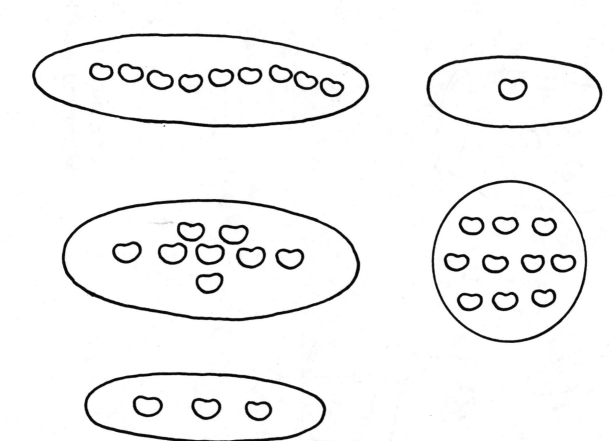

Soccer Time!

Skill Time

Getting Started

Set a large clock with moveable hands to 9:00. Ask children to tell the time shown on the clock. Then invite them to tell about what activities they do at that time of day? What do they do at that time of night? Invite a volunteer to pantomime an activity that might be performed at that time of the day or night. Ask the class to guess the activity and tell whether it is usually a daytime or nighttime activity (or both, in some cases). Then reset the clock to a different hour and repeat the activity. Continue until you have covered every hour of the day.

Completing the Mini-Book

Ask children to write their name on the cover, then cut out and glue the patterns onto the pages, as shown. Finally, have them complete the activity on the last page.

Reproducible Pages
mini-book:
pages 90–95
patterns:
page 96

Write the time shown on each watch.

Taking It Further

Play a game of Time Memory. To prepare, stamp analog clock faces onto 8-10 plain index cards. Draw hands on the clocks to show different times to the hour. Then create another set of cards that show the corresponding digital times. To play, mix up the cards and place them facedown on a table. Invite children to take turns flipping over two cards at a time. If the cards show the same time, they keep the cards. If not, they return the cards facedown and the next player takes a turn.

I ♥ Soccer

Tick tock.

It is time to wake up.

Anna's watch says **7:00**.

Soccer Time!

by _____

Tick tock.

It is time to eat breakfast.

Jay's watch says **8:00**.

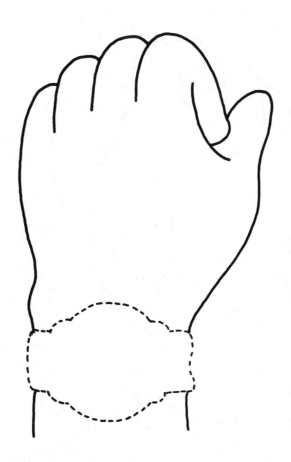

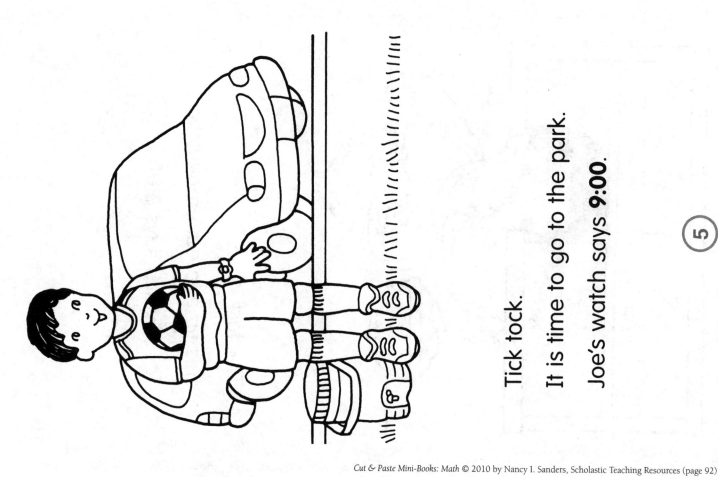

Tick tock.

It is time to go to the park.

Joe's watch says **9:00**.

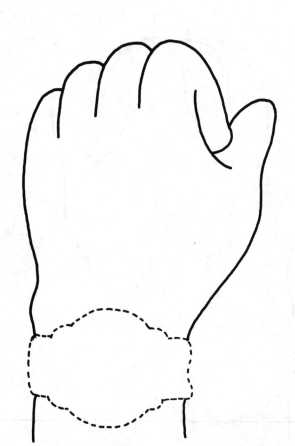

Tick tock.

It is time for the game.

The coach's watch says **10:00**.

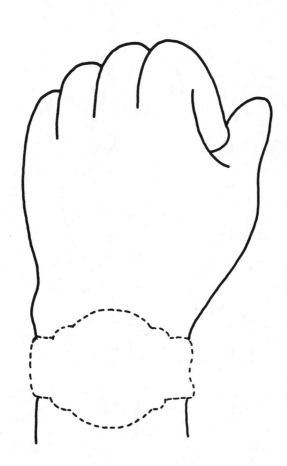

Tick tock.

It is time for our pizza party!

Becky's watch says **12:00.**

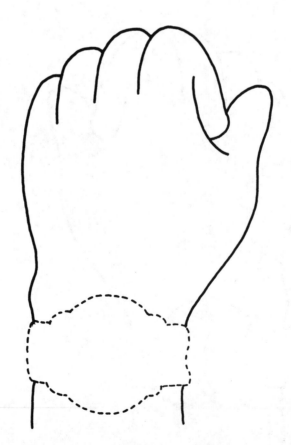

Write the time shown on each watch.

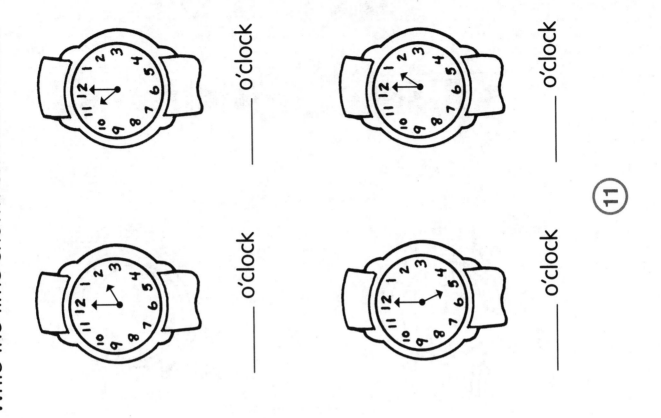

_____ o'clock

_____ o'clock

_____ o'clock

_____ o'clock

Cut & Paste Mini-Books: Math © 2010 by Nancy I. Sanders, Scholastic Teaching Resources (page 95)

(11)

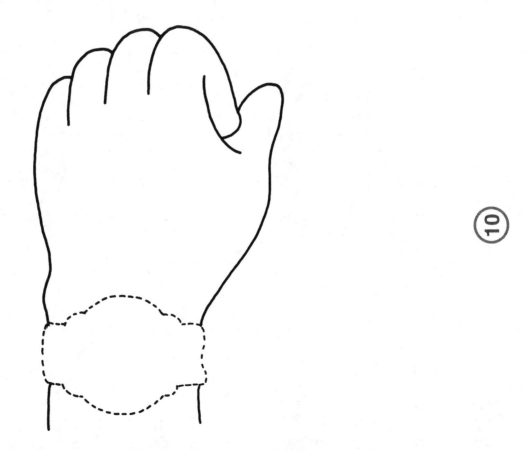

(10)

Soccer Time

Cut & Paste Patterns

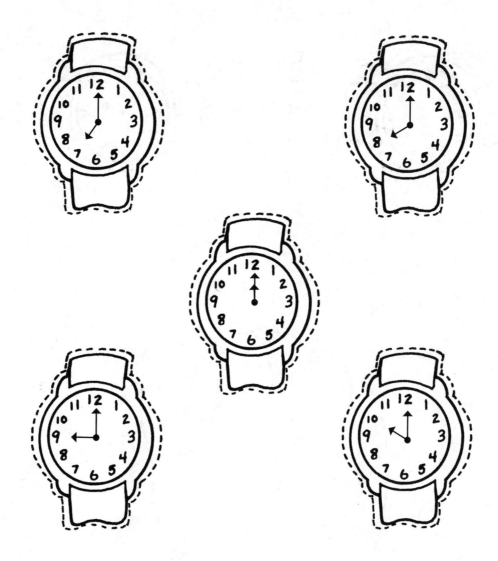

My Fat Cat, Sam

Skill Calendar Concepts

Getting Started

Use a pocket chart with clear pockets to help familiarize children with the order of the days of the week. On three separate sentence strips write "Yesterday was _____," "Today is _____," and "Tomorrow will be _____." Then cut seven sentence strips to fit the blanks in the sentences. Write a different day of the week on each strip. Place the sentence strips in the pocket chart and display it near your class calendar. Keep the word cards nearby. Each day during calendar time, invite a volunteer to put the appropriate word cards into the pocket chart to complete each sentence.

Completing the Mini-Book

Ask children to write their name on the cover, then cut out and glue the patterns onto the pages, as shown. Finally, have them complete the activity on the last page.

Reproducible Pages
mini-book: pages 98–103
patterns: page 104

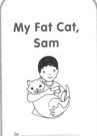

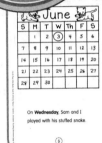

Trace the letters and say the days.

Taking It Further

Use show-and-tell time to reinforce the days of the week. First, form five groups—one for each day from Monday through Friday. Assign each group a symbol, such as apples, stars, or boats. To prepare a calendar for the current month, attach each group's symbol to all of the days of the week assigned to that group. (Removable stickers work well.) Then have children check the calendar for their symbol to see on which day they will share during show-and-tell.

S	M	T	W	Th	F	S
	(1)	2	3	4	5	6
7	8	9	10	11	12	13
14	15	16	17	18	19	20
21	22	23	24	25	26	27
28	29	30				

June

I like to play with my

fat cat named Sam.

On **Monday**, Sam and I

played with his ball of yarn.

(1)

My Fat Cat, Sam

by _____

June

S	M	T	W	Th	F	S
	1	(2)	3	4	5	6
7	8	9	10	11	12	13
14	15	16	17	18	19	20
21	22	23	24	25	26	27
28	29	30				

On **Tuesday**, Sam and I played with his toy mouse.

③

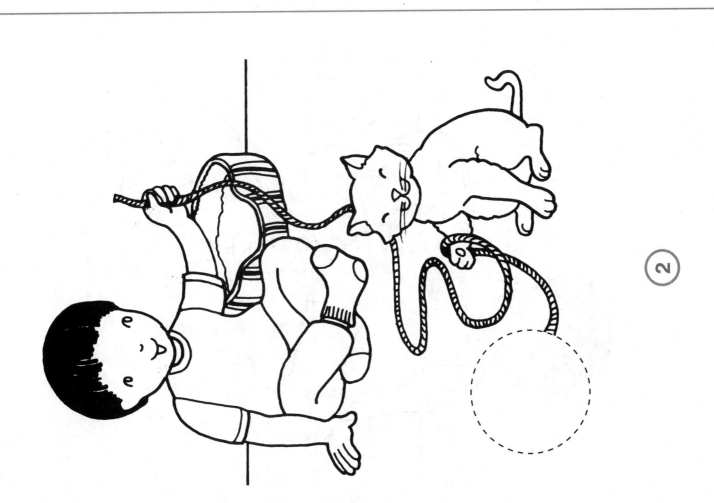

②

S	M	T	W	Th	F	S
June						
	1	2	③	4	5	6
7	8	9	10	11	12	13
14	15	16	17	18	19	20
21	22	23	24	25	26	27
28	29	30				

On **Wednesday**, Sam and I played with his stuffed snake.

Cut & Paste Mini-Books: Math © 2010 by Nancy I. Sanders, Scholastic Teaching Resources (page 100)

5

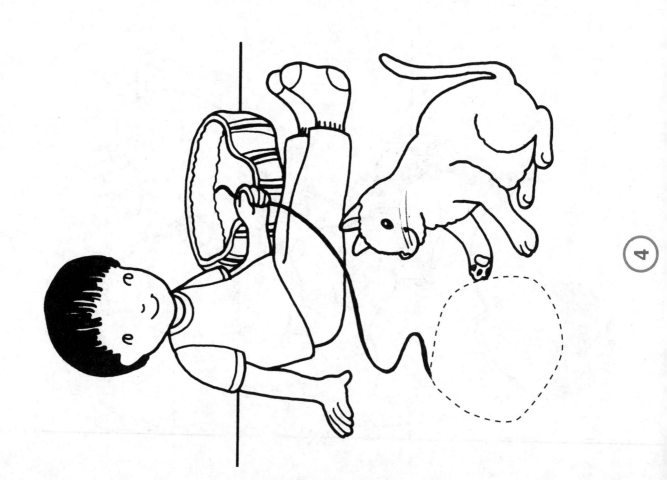

4

June

S	M	T	W	Th	F	S
	1	2	3	(4)	5	6
7	8	9	10	11	12	13
14	15	16	17	18	19	20
21	22	23	24	25	26	27
28	29	30				

On **Thursday,** Sam and I
played with his feather toy.

7

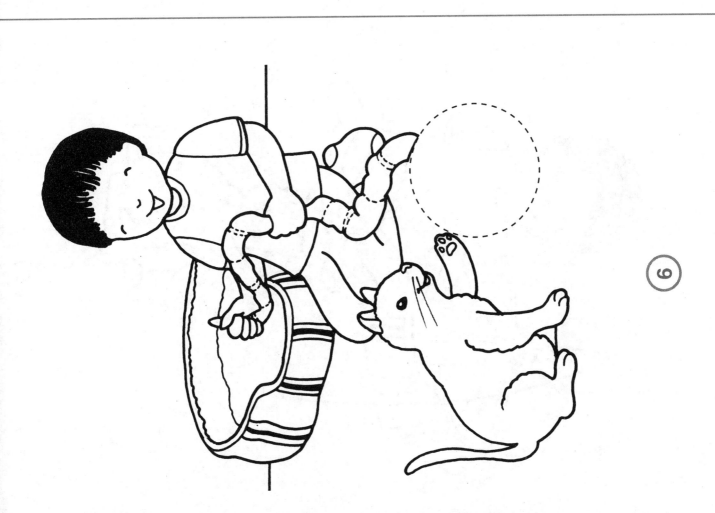

6

June

S	M	T	W	Th	F	S
	1	2	3	4	(5)	6
7	8	9	10	11	12	13
14	15	16	17	18	19	20
21	22	23	24	25	26	27
28	29	30				

On **Friday**, I got a surprise.

Sam had 3 kittens!

Now my cat is not fat.

And she has a new name—Sammi!

⑨

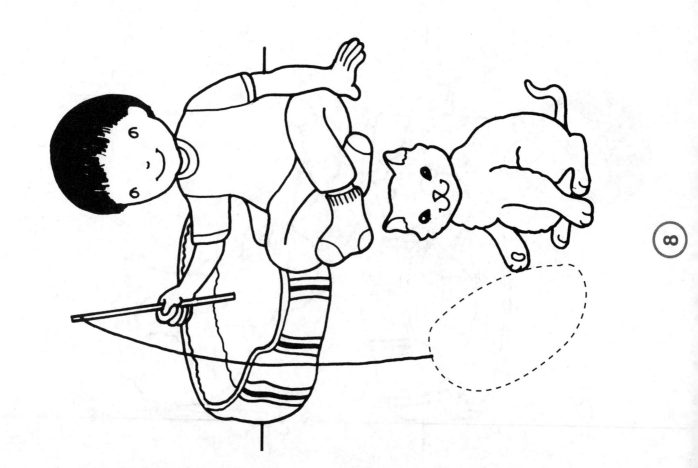

⑧

Trace the letters.
Say the days.

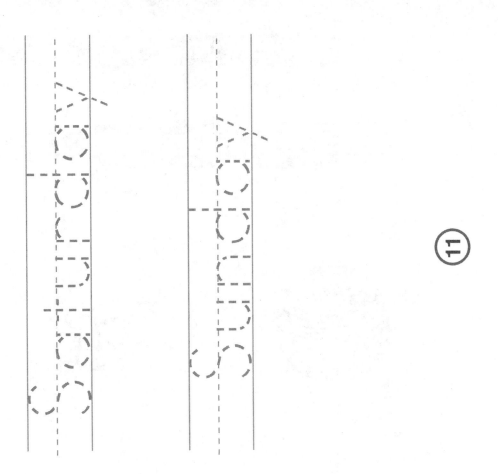

Cut & Paste Mini-Books: Math © 2010 by Nancy I. Sanders, Scholastic Teaching Resources (page 103)

My Fat Cat, Sam

Cut & Paste Patterns

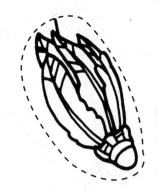

Claire's Coins

Skill · Money

Getting Started

Provide children with plastic or cardboard pennies, nickels, and dimes. Hold up each type of coin and ask children to identify it and its value. Afterward, have children compare the coins (their color, size, and shape). Then create coin combinations for children to duplicate with their own set of coins. Have them tell the value of each combination. After several rounds of practice, name different money amounts and have children create coin combinations for each amount.

Completing the Mini-Book

Ask children to write their name on the cover, then cut out and glue the patterns onto the pages, as shown. Finally, have them complete the activity on the last page.

Reproducible Pages
mini-book:
pages 106–111

patterns:
page 112

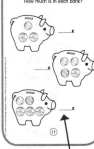

Write the amount of money in each bank.

Taking It Further

Invite children to draw a purse or wallet on paper. Provide coin stamps or copies of coins for children to cut out. Ask them to stamp or glue several coins of their choice onto their drawing. Then instruct them to find the value of the coin combination and write that amount at the top of their paper. Finally, encourage children to write a sentence or short story at the bottom telling how they would use their coins. Invite them to share their work with the class.

Hip, hip, hooray!

Claire is counting coins today!

She counts **5¢** plus **3¢**.

She has _____ ¢ in a bank.

Cut & Paste Mini-Books: Math © 2010 by Nancy I. Sanders, Scholastic Teaching Resources (page 106)

Claire's Coins

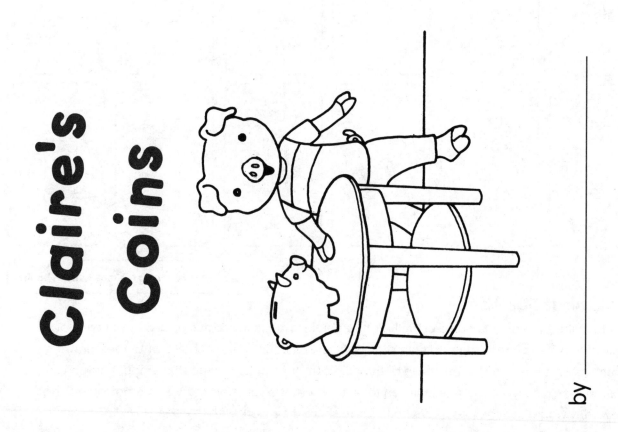

by _____

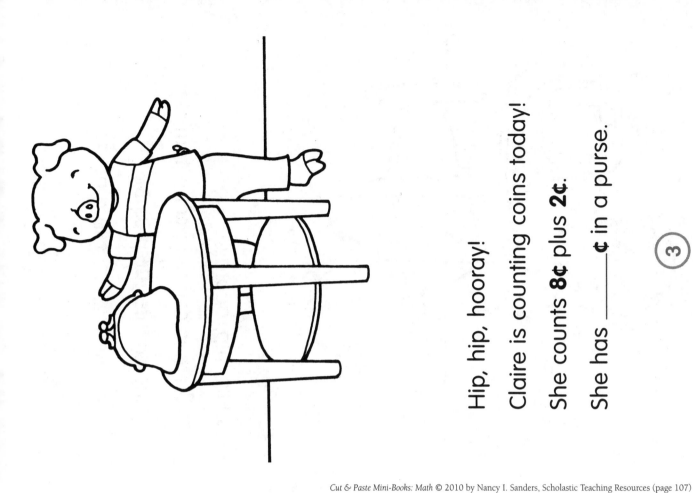

Hip, hip, hooray!

Claire is counting coins today!

She counts **8¢** plus **2¢**.

She has ——— **¢** in a purse.

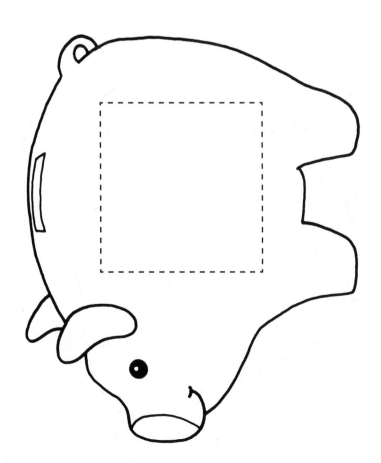

Hip, hip, hooray!

Claire is counting coins today!

She counts **10¢** plus **5¢**.

She has _____ **¢** in a pocket.

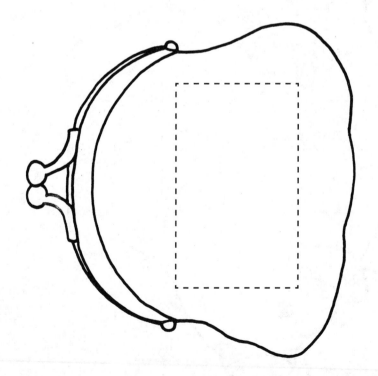

4

Hip, hip, hooray!

Claire is counting coins today!

She counts **15¢** plus **4¢**.

She has _____ **¢** in a dish.

(7)

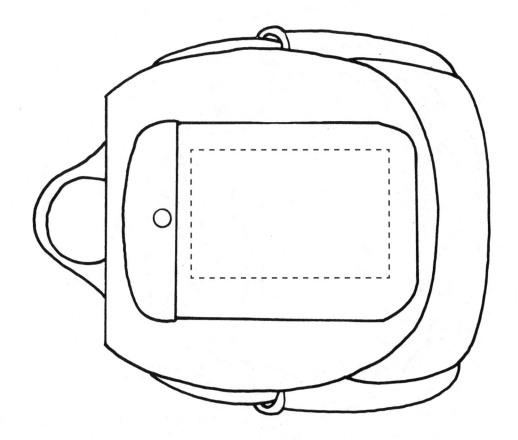

Hip, hip, hooray!

Claire is counting coins today!

She counts **19¢** plus **6¢**.

She has _____ ¢ in a jar.

Now she'll put it away

for a rainy day!

Cut & Paste Mini-Books: Math © 2010 by Nancy I. Sanders, Scholastic Teaching Resources (page 110)

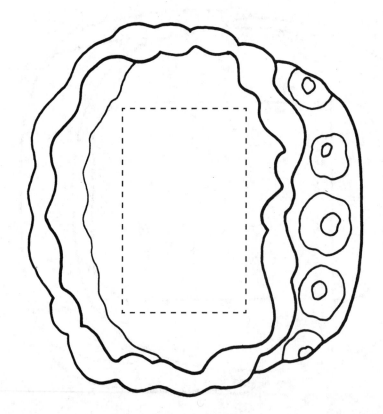

How much is in each bank?

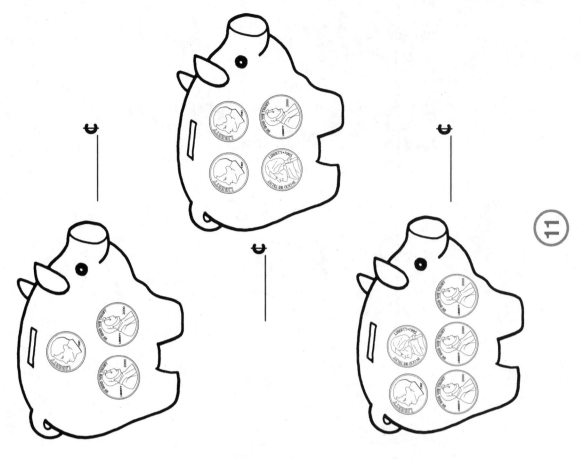

¢

¢

¢

¢

11

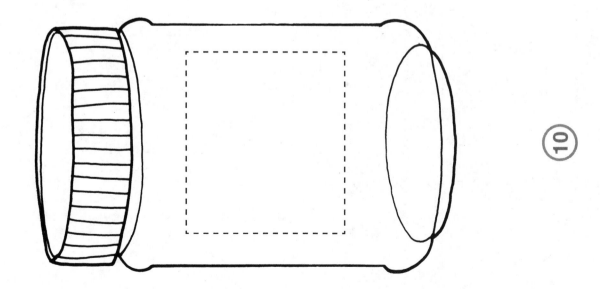

10

Claire's Coins

Cut & Paste Patterns

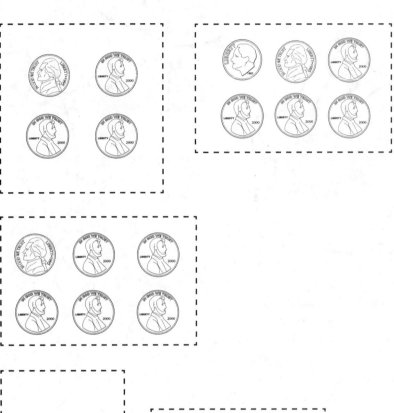

Cut & Paste Mini-Books: Math © 2010 by Nancy I. Sanders, Scholastic Teaching Resources

The Bake Shop

Getting Started

Provide children with four sheets of plain paper. Have them fold one sheet in half, another into fourths, one into thirds, and the last one into sixths. Then have them unfold their papers to reveal the equal sections created by the folds. Explain how each section is an equal part of the whole sheet of paper. Help children name each fractional part of their papers. Finally, write various fractions on the board. Have children name each fraction and place markers on the sections of their papers to represent that fraction.

Completing the Mini-Book

Ask children to write their name on the cover, then cut out and glue the patterns onto the pages, as shown. Finally, have them complete the activity on the last page.

Reproducible Pages
mini-book:
pages 114–119
patterns:
page 120

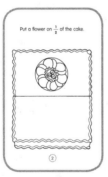
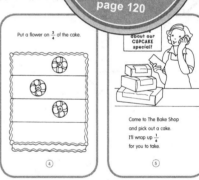

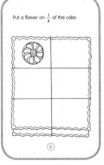

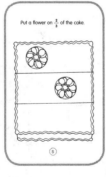

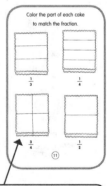

Color the part of each cake to match the fraction.

Taking It Further

Cut several sheets of construction paper into equal fractional parts to represent "cakes" that have been cut into same-sized slices (fourths, sixths, and so on). Then prepare a supply of die-cut flowers. To use, mix up all the parts belonging to two different cakes. Pair up children and ask the partners to assemble each cake. Then have one child name a fractional part of one of the cakes, such as 3/4 or 2/6, and have the other put flowers on the pieces to represent that fraction.

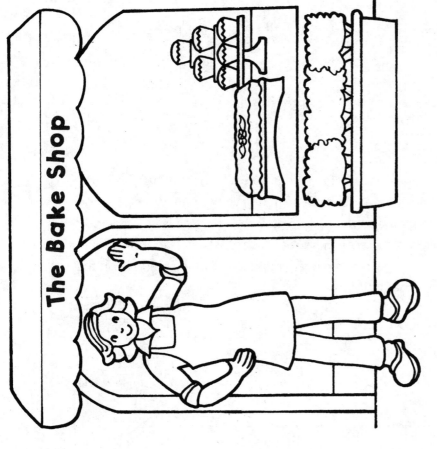

The Bake Shop

Come to The Bake Shop
and pick out a cake.

I'll wrap up $\frac{1}{2}$

for you to take.

Cut & Paste Mini-Books: Math © 2010 by Nancy I. Sanders, Scholastic Teaching Resources (page 114)

The Bake Shop

by _____

Come to The Bake Shop
and pick out a cake.
I'll wrap up $\frac{3}{4}$
for you to take.

Put a flower on $\frac{1}{2}$ of the cake.

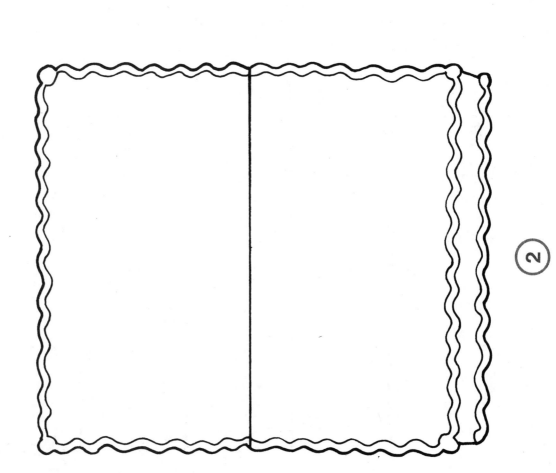

②

Ask me about our CUPCAKE special!

Come to The Bake Shop
and pick out a cake.
I'll wrap up $\frac{1}{6}$
for you to take.

⑤

Cut & Paste Mini-Books: Math © 2010 by Nancy I. Sanders, Scholastic Teaching Resources (page 116)

Put a flower on $\frac{3}{4}$ of the cake.

④

Come to The Bake Shop
and pick out a cake.

I'll wrap up $\frac{2}{3}$
for you to take.

Put a flower on $\frac{1}{6}$ of the cake.

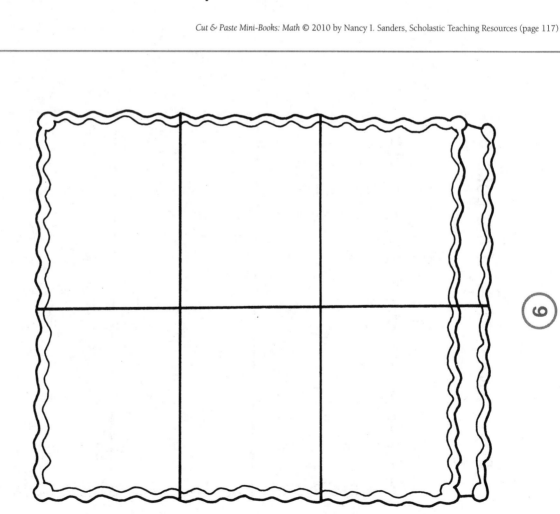

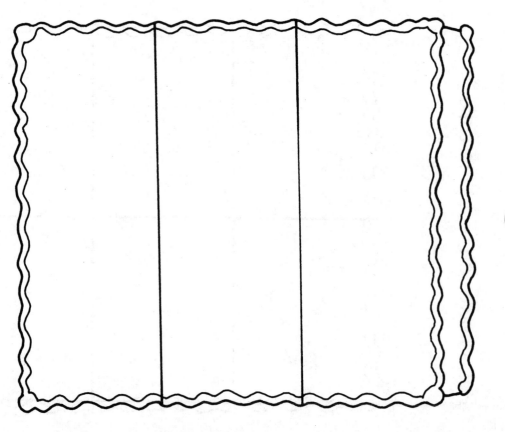

Come to The Bake Shop
and pick out a cake.

I'll wrap up $\frac{1}{4}$
for you to take.

Put a flower on $\frac{2}{3}$ of the cake.

Color the part of each cake
to match the fraction.

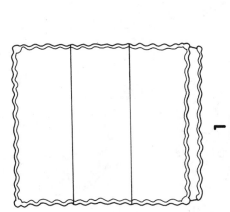

$\frac{1}{4}$

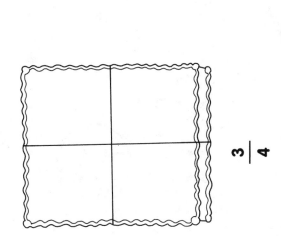

$\frac{1}{3}$

$\frac{1}{2}$

$\frac{3}{4}$

Cut & Paste Mini-Books: Math © 2010 by Nancy I. Sanders, Scholastic Teaching Resources (page 119)

(11)

Put a flower on $\frac{1}{4}$ of the cake.

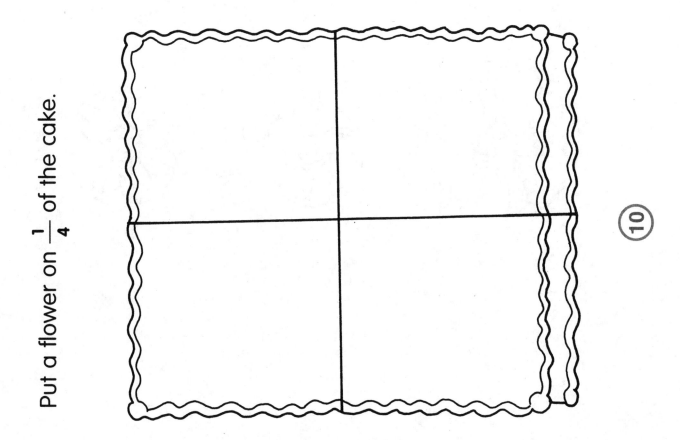

(10)

The Bake Shop

Cut & Paste Patterns

Who Lives on Fairy Tale Lane?

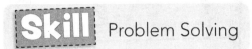

Skill Problem Solving

Getting Started

Cut out three simple construction-paper houses. Draw a different combination of windows and doors on each house (use different shapes and a different number of windows and doors on the houses). Display the houses in a clear pocket chart and name the shape of each window and door. Then make up logic problems about the houses for children to solve. For example, you might ask them to find the house that has a rectangle door and fewer than two windows. If desired, create additional houses and switch them around to create more and varied problems.

Completing the Mini-Book

Ask children to write their name on the cover, then cut out and glue the patterns onto the pages, as shown. Finally, have them complete the activity on the last page.

Reproducible Pages
mini-book: pages 122–127
patterns: page 128

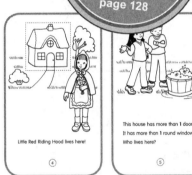

Circle the house described.

Taking It Further

Pair up children and give each pair a small paper cup. Have each pair count out 11 pieces of popcorn into its cup. Explain that the partners will take turns removing one to three pieces of popcorn from the cup, with the goal of forcing the other person to take the last piece. As they play, invite children to explain their strategy. After the cup is empty, invite the partners to eat the popcorn they removed and then refill their cup for another round.

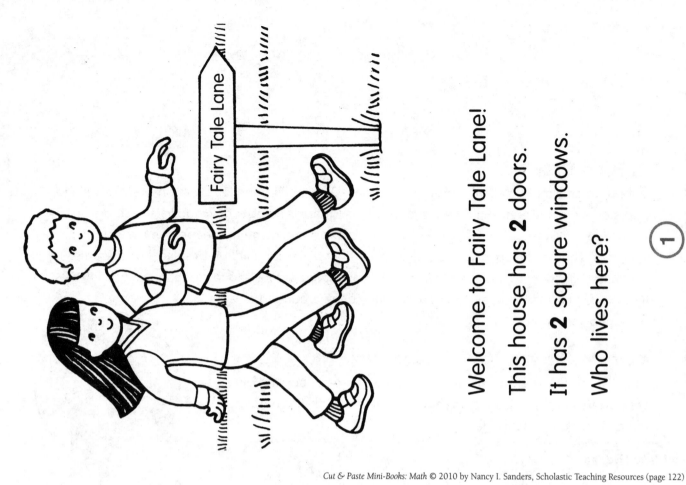

Welcome to Fairy Tale Lane!

This house has **2** doors.

It has **2** square windows.

Who lives here?

Who Lives on Fairy Tale Lane?

by _____

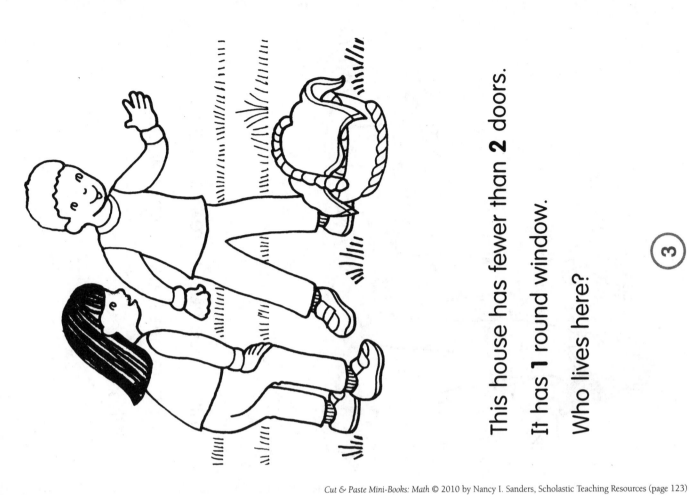

This house has fewer than **2** doors.

It has **1** round window.

Who lives here?

③

Cut & Paste Mini-Books: Math © 2010 by Nancy I. Sanders, Scholastic Teaching Resources (page 123)

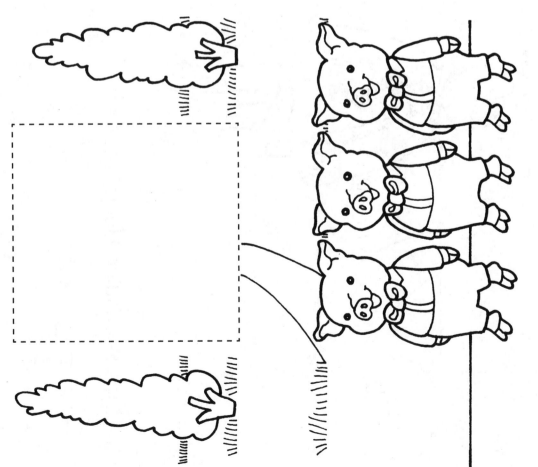

The three little pigs live here!

②

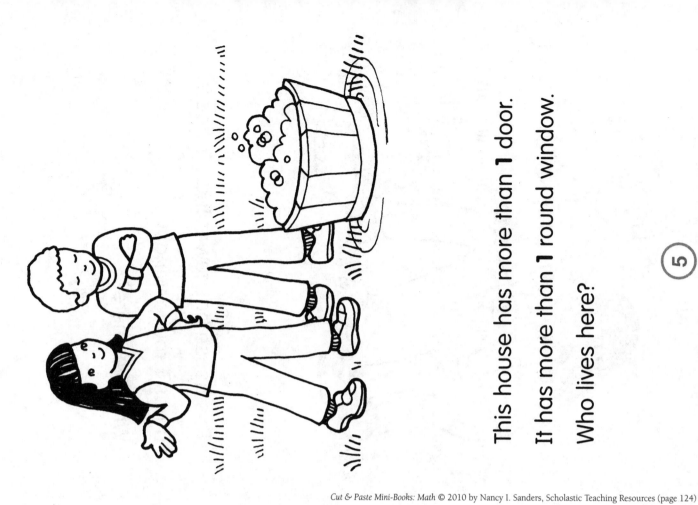

This house has more than **1** door.

It has more than **1** round window.

Who lives here?

Cut & Paste Mini-Books: Math © 2010 by Nancy I. Sanders, Scholastic Teaching Resources (page 124)

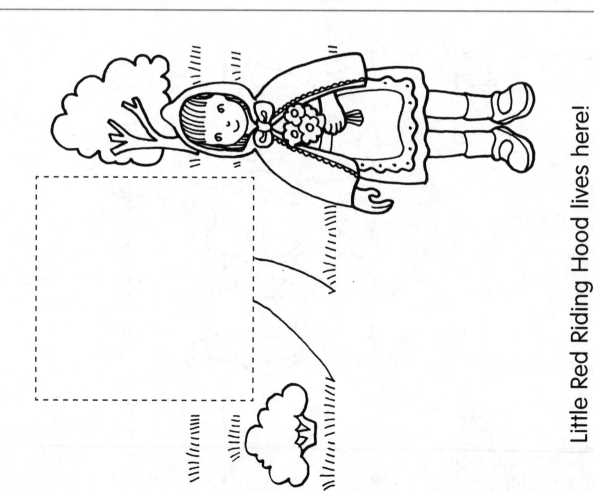

Little Red Riding Hood lives here!

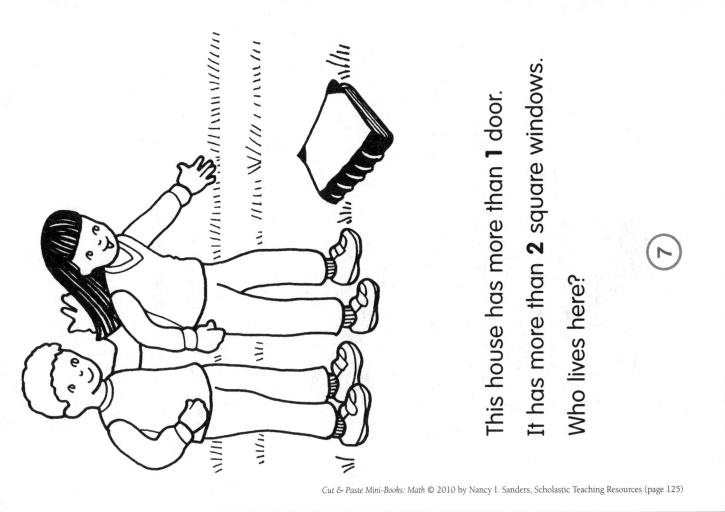

This house has more than **1** door.

It has more than **2** square windows.

Who lives here?

⑦

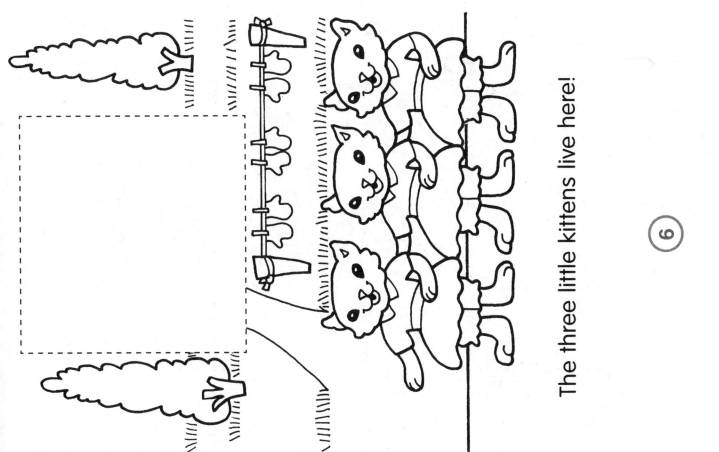

The three little kittens live here!

⑥

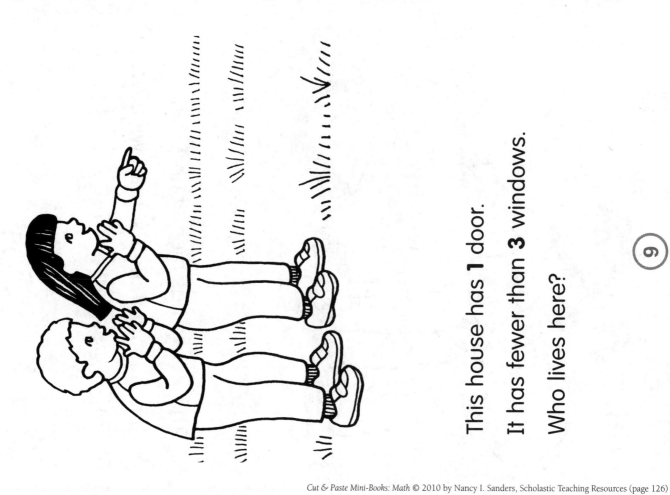

This house has **1** door.

It has fewer than **3** windows.

Who lives here?

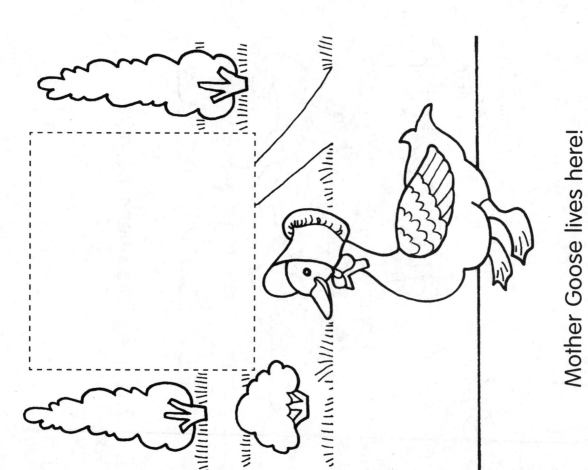

Mother Goose lives here!

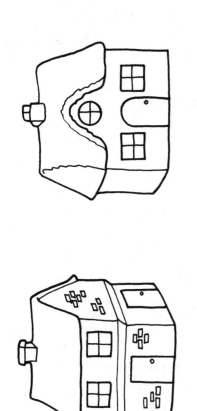

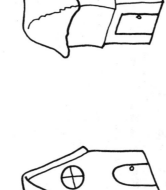

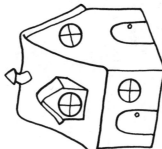

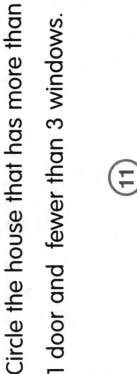

Circle the house that has more than 1 door and fewer than 3 windows.

(11)

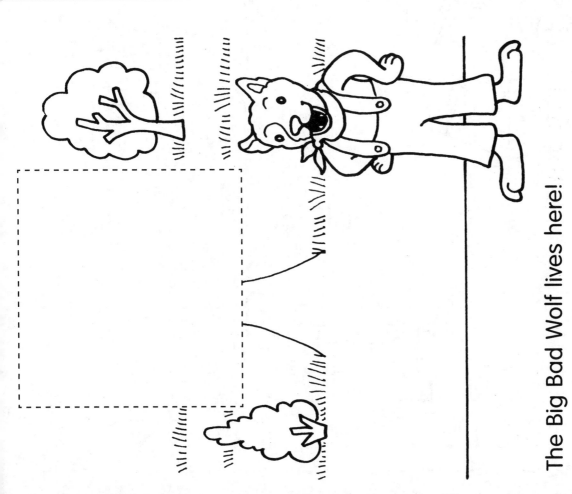

The Big Bad Wolf lives here!

Uh-oh, it's time to leave Fairy Tale Lane!

(10)

Who Lives on Fairy Tale Lane?

Cut & Paste Patterns